Fast Forward

Confessions of a Porn Screenwriter

Fast Forward

Confessions of a Porn Screenwriter

Eric Spitznagel

the Future Tense series

Manic D Press
San Francisco

Published by Manic D Press, Inc., P.O. Box 410804, San Francisco, CA 94141.
www.manicdpress.com Printed in the USA

Future Tense editor: Kevin Sampsell
Cover design: Scott Idleman/BLINK Production assistant: Risa Kahn

Portions of this book previously appeared in a slightly different form in *Hitch* magazine, Salon.com, Pif.com, and *3AM* magazine.

While this book is based on a true story, some elements have been exaggerated, embellished, and (at times) outright fabricated. The author leaves the distinction up to the reader's imagination. Excluding publicly-known figures, who in no way endorse or otherwise approve of this memoir, all names have been changed to protect the innocent and heavily armed.

Library of Congress Cataloging-in-Publication Data

Spitznagel, Eric.
Fast forward : confessions of a porn screenwriter / Eric Spitznagel.
p. cm.
Summary: "A humorous behind-the-scenes account of the pornographic film industry, as seen through the eyes of one of its writers."--Provided by the publisher.
ISBN-13: 978-1-933149-05-9 (trade pbk.)
ISBN-10: 1-933149-05-1 (trade pbk.)
1. Screenwriters--Fiction. 2. Sex-oriented businesses--Fiction.
3. Pornography--Fiction. 4. Motion picture industry--Fiction.
5. Hollywood (Los Angeles, Calif.)--Fiction. I. Title.
PS3619.P59F37 2006
813'.6--dc22

2006007709

To my Dad,
who taught me how to laugh at everything

“Sometimes the stars shine more brightly
seen from the gutter than from the hilltop.”
— *W. Somerset Maughm*

“He’s a fine writer, but
I wouldn’t want to shake hands with him.”
— *Jacqueline Susann, on Philip Roth*

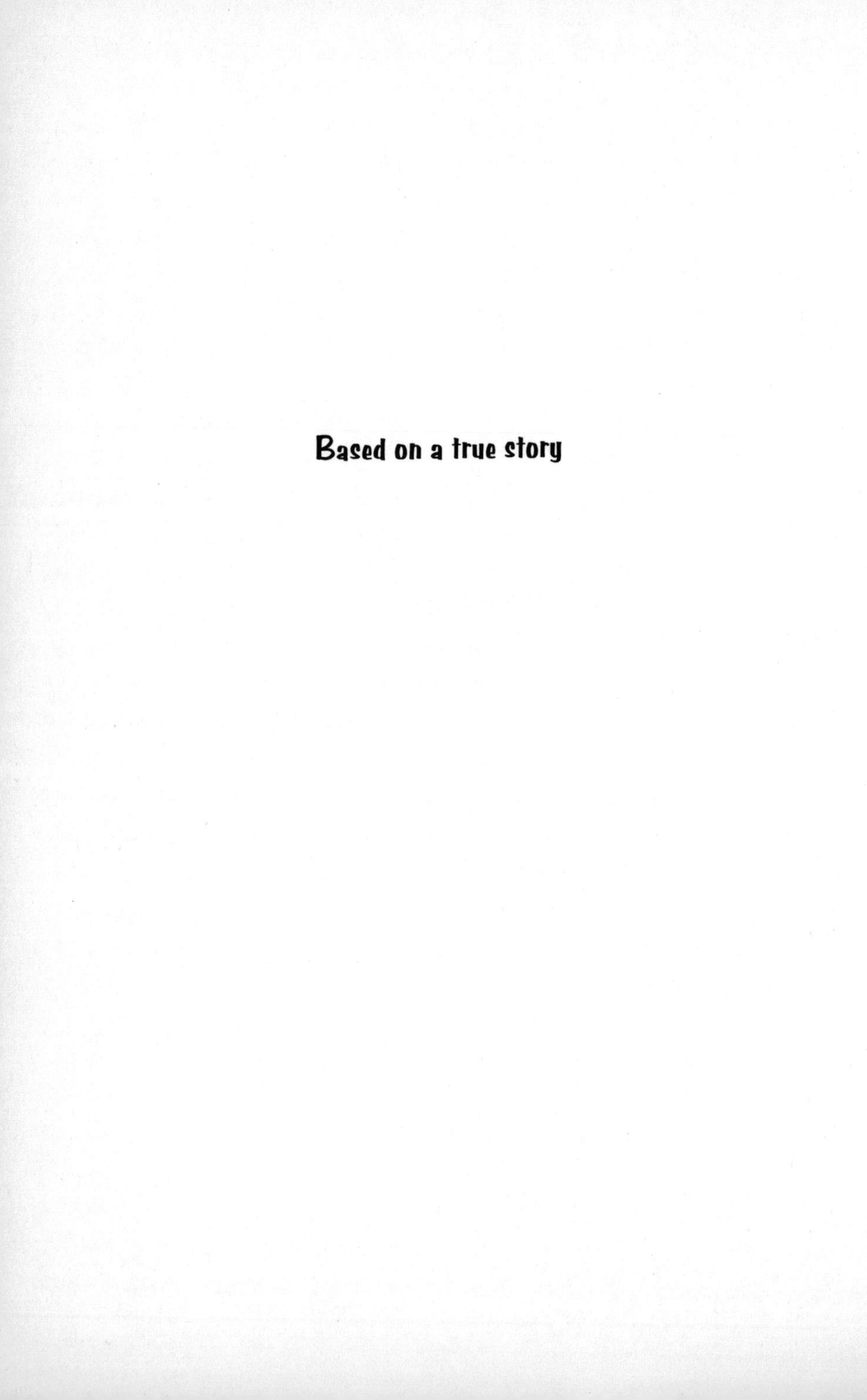

Based on a true story

1

"Have you ever thought about writing a porno?"

At first, I was fairly sure that Tim was joking. He had a healthy sense of humor about the screenwriting trade, of which we were both would-be members. When our prospects of finding meaningful employment seemed particularly bleak (which was invariably), we would often joke about selling out to the porn industry. For some reason, we always found this terribly amusing, and in a way, strangely comforting. I suppose the ridiculous concept of peddling smut for a living made the shadow of poverty seem a little less terrifying.

"Well... sure," I said, with a mocking grin. "That's why I moved to L.A."

Tim didn't return my smile. He peered at me with a somber expression and extinguished his cigarette into a plate of untouched eggs, already piled high with butts.

We were sitting in a mostly empty coffeeshop in West

Hollywood. It had been Tim's idea to meet here, and judging by the urgency in his voice when he'd called, I assumed it was important. During our days as struggling writers in Chicago, we'd promised that if either of us made it, we would find a way to share the wealth. Although I'd only been in Los Angeles for a few weeks, Tim had lived here for almost two years and had a considerable head start on me. I suppose I thought he would have something substantial to offer me by now. If not a real career opportunity, then at least an insider tip. Something to get me started. I certainly expected more from him than sniggering remarks about porn.

"I'm serious," he said. "It's not as bad as it sounds. The money's pretty good, and it's certainly better than a day job."

I couldn't believe what I was hearing. One of my dearest friends was actually advising me to do the unspeakable, to venture into the darkest underbelly of Hollywood. Porn was the final destination for teenage runaways and high school dropouts with dreams of celluloid glory. I never considered that a writer might fall into the oily grasp of pornographers. It just didn't happen that way. A broke writer may turn to journalism or even, God forbid, advertising. But never porn.

"Are you actually considering this?" I was incredulous.

"Oh, I'm not considering," he said. "I've already done it."

He told me the whole ugly story. It began just months ago, when he'd gone to the Sundance Film Festival with hopes of landing a film deal. After passing out his business card to anybody even vaguely associated with a major studio, it looked as if he would be leaving empty-handed. But on his last night in town, he attended an after-hours party where a friend of a friend of a friend introduced him to a porn director. A few hundred cocktails later, his judgment skills sufficiently impaired, he'd been hired to write his first feature-length screenplay.

"I finished it in one afternoon," he said. "Twenty pages for five hundred bucks. It's the best money I've ever made."

"You're not using your real name, are you?" I asked.

"No, of course not."

"Aren't you afraid that somebody will find out?"

Tim just laughed. "And how would they do that? You think anybody actually pays attention to a porno's production credits?"

"Yeah, but—"

"It's not like I'm putting my reputation on the line here. Nobody is going to watch this thing and think less of me as a writer. Odds are, nobody will even remember it."

He had a point. I'd watched more than a few pornos in my time, and couldn't recall a single plot. And why should I? Like any man my age, my libido suffered from a short attention span. And porn offered the ultimate experience in instant gratification. It was the perfect sexual release for anybody with a few hours to kill and working knowledge of the fast forward button.

"You know," he said, "a lot of famous writers started out in porn."

"Name one," I challenged.

"Jerry Stahl."

He had me there. Stahl's brief stint as a porn screenwriter was legendary, at least in certain literary circles. The prolific scribe of sitcoms like *Alf* and *Moonlighting* had indeed written several adult films during his early days in Hollywood, and he'd made no attempt to conceal it. He'd discussed his experiences in countless interviews, and documented it in his autobiography, *Permanent Midnight*. Stranger still, his porn beginnings had not hurt his career, and had helped elevate him to the level of hipster icon.

"Stahl isn't the half of it,"Tim continued."Barry Sonnenfeld also started out in porn. So did Wes Craven and Richard LaGravanese. You see what I'm saying? If they could get away with it, there's no reason why I can't. I should be so lucky to have their careers."

I wanted to be disgusted with him. A writer in L.A. was supposed to endure poverty, suffer with quiet nobility while he waited for Hollywood to recognize his genius and reward him accordingly. But Tim had sold out in the worst possible way. He had settled for less, gorged himself on chum in the water. He was wasting his talents on an industry with no cultural significance, a creative black hole where ideas go to die. How could one of my friends — one of my *peers* — have been so easily duped?

But honestly, I was angry because I hadn't thought of it first.

It was never my idea to move to L.A. That had been my wife's doing. She decided, quite abruptly, that she wanted to try her hand at writing sitcoms. I would have been happy just to stay in Chicago: I was born there, I'd spent most of my life there, and had every reason to believe that I would die there someday. But my wife insisted that Chicago was career suicide for a writer, so we left. I guess I could have put up more of a fight, but a part of me wanted her to be happy, and a bigger part of me wanted to be married to a TV writer who regularly made obscene amounts of money. Despite a long-standing hatred of all things West Coast, we packed up our meager belongings and set out for sunny California.

For as long as I can remember, I've been a proud armchair critic of Hollywood, regularly coughing up tired old clichés like "L.A. has no culture" and "It isn't normal to live in a city without seasons." But after we moved there, my opinions about California's nether region changed radically. This is not to suggest that my paranoid assumptions about L.A. proved to be inaccurate. It has no culture, the weather is redundant at best, and everybody who lives there is, exactly as I suspected, a raging egomaniac. So how, you may be asking, could any person possibly fall in love with a city so inherently evil? Wasn't there the least concern that this move would result in the eternal damnation of my creative soul?

It doesn't take much for a man's principles to be conveniently tossed aside. For me, it was as simple as one phone call from an L.A. agent.

"You are, hands down, the most talented writer of your generation," he told me. "I kid you not. I've never met anybody with more potential for greatness. If you give me the chance, I'm going to make you a star. I guarantee it. You sign with us, and you'll have your first million within the year."

As a humor writer, having my ass kissed so shamelessly was a bit disconcerting. Accustomed to a lifetime of obscurity and small paychecks, I never imagined that I could hope for anything more. I certainly never expected to have one of the largest agencies in Los Angeles call up out of the blue and promise the world. There had to be a catch but I couldn't, for the life of me, figure out what it might be. It seemed peculiar that anybody in his position would want to represent me, given the fact that I had never written a screenplay, nor had any inclinations to do so. But he was insistent, and I couldn't very well refuse someone so unwavering in his admiration.

I was invited to numerous breakfast meetings to discuss my impending fame. Meeting at posh diners throughout Beverly

Hills, I was force-fed omelets and cappuccinos. He said that studios were already lining up to make a deal, and that I should keep my schedule clear should they need me to begin work immediately. It seemed too good to be true, but far be it from me to complain. As long as the free meals kept coming and my ego was getting stroked on a regular basis, I was happy just to sit back and enjoy the ride.

It wasn't until our fourth meeting that my agent dropped a bombshell: "Where's the script?"

This was the first time that he'd mentioned an actual screenplay. After all the assurances of instant glory and riches, it'd never crossed my mind that I might be expected to write something. Maybe I thought I'd just be handed a check for my biting wit and charming sensibilities.

"I need a script," the agent said, getting snippy. "There's nothing I can do for you until I have a script."

So I wrote one. I'm not sure how it got done so quickly. Maybe it was inspiration, but more likely I just felt obligated to satisfy this man who seemed to be riding his entire financial future on my abilities. Days after the first draft was delivered, the agent called again and began filling my head with more visions of dollar signs. The script was perfect, he said. A veritable work of genius. It was disturbing that he'd been so easily pleased, but his enthusiasm was intoxicating, and I became even more convinced that my success was a foregone conclusion.

And then one day, the calls stopped coming.

I wasn't particularly concerned, and just assumed that he was too busy pitching my script or negotiating my million-dollar contract. Days passed. And the days turned to weeks. I called, but he always seemed to be in a meeting or out to lunch. Voicemail messages were left and e-mails sent, but he never responded. I felt like a college co-ed who'd been seduced by a frat boy only to be brushed aside after he'd had his way with her.

I called my New York agent (with whom a healthy relationship has continued, if only because of his tendency to return my calls) and complained to him about my predicament, but he wasn't nearly as pessimistic. "That's just the way they do things in L.A.," he told me. "Don't take it personally."

I tried to take his advice, but that was easier said than done when rent must be paid and a promised fortune has kept you from seeking meaningful employment. I was flat broke—and if my luck didn't change soon—on the verge of being homeless.

Welcome to L.A.

When I arrived home later that day, I couldn't resist telling my wife about Tim's porn misadventures, feeling like a giggling older brother tattling on the misdeeds of a younger sibling. I took a mean-spirited delight in relaying every juicy detail, and fully expected her to share my enthusiasm. It was a horrible thing to do, I know, but we both needed a distraction from our stalled careers.

My wife didn't find it nearly as amusing. In fact, she had the audacity to suggest that Tim might be onto something. Maybe, she said, I should be following his lead, and might consider how I too could become a professional porn scribe.

"Are you out of your mind?" I replied, unable to conceal my moral outrage.

"Well, why not?" she said. "It'll give you something productive to do with your time. What have you got to lose? It's better than lying around the house all day. And it's not like you've been getting any other offers."

She was obviously making allusions to the agent, who may or may not have dumped me. Hurt by her insinuation, I insisted, "He's going to call. I'm just going to give it a few more days."

"It's not like anybody is asking you to make a career of this. Just write the script, get some quick cash, and that'll be the end of it. Who knows? It may be fun."

"I don't see you volunteering to do this," I muttered.

"Hey, thus far I'm the only one making some honest money around here. It's about time you started pulling your weight."

Of course, it wasn't necessary to mention that she wasn't having any better luck in her chosen career path. To her credit, she had come closer than I had to finding an actual job in the entertainment field. After obtaining an agent, she had managed to secure meetings with various TV producers. But we had somehow timed our move to L.A. so that it perfectly coincided with a writers' strike. She'd been assured of her talents, but told in no uncertain terms that she would not be able to secure employment for at least the next one to two years.

In the meantime, she'd found a few other jobs to pay the bills. Now, when I say "jobs" I mean, of course, "game shows." Since we'd moved to L.A., she'd been a contestant on more than four game shows. And yet despite all her efforts, she had only $300 and a synthesizer to show for it. Not exactly the big bucks we'd been hoping for, but then again, beggars can't be choosers. Of course, beggars can't buy food with a synthesizer either, but who's counting, right?

"You really think I should do this?" I asked her.

"Why not?" she replied. "If nothing else, it'll make for great talk show fodder."

"What do you mean?"

"One of these days, you're going to hit it big. And when

you're doing the talk show circuit, you're going to need some amusing anecdotes. You mean to tell me you've never thought about this?"

I was too ashamed to admit that the thought had never crossed my mind. Like any self-respecting writer, I'd been fine-tuning my Pulitzer Prize acceptance speech for most of my life. I'd also done a little work on my imminent podium time at the Oscars and Golden Globes. I even had a Grammy speech tucked away somewhere, just to be on the safe side. But I'd never once considered the possibility of appearing on a talk show.

"Just think about it," she continued. "You're sitting on the couch next to Dave or Jay, and you mention how you used to write porn for a living. I'm telling you, they'll eat it up."

I had to admit, she might be onto something. The money was one thing, but if writing porn could result in at least one colorful yarn, suitable for any number of talk shows and magazine interviews, then I owed it to myself—to my *career*—to take this chance. If I didn't do it for myself, I should at least do it for Dave.

As I sat down to write my first porn screenplay, I established one rule: I could not take more than an afternoon to complete it. If I gave it more attention than that, I was obviously giving the thing too much thought. This was not rocket science, after all. It wasn't even remedial physics. It was *porn*. "Pizza guy knocks on door, big-breasted woman in flimsy negligee answers, they have sex." Bing-boom-done.

If I was at all tentative, it was because I wasn't entirely sure how to write a porno sex scene. Just how much information would I be expected to provide? Would every sexual act need to be choreographed: exactly where each limb should be placed, which bits should be inserted into which orifice like some perverse VCR operator's manual? Though I was confident in my abilities as a writer, I'd never attempted to summarize the mechanics of sexual congress. If it in any way resembled the literary porn I was familiar with, it would necessitate a vast arsenal of erotic adjectives, and it was doubtful if I could come up with anything more provocative than "pulsating."

Tim was kind enough to loan me a copy of his screenplay, and my fears quickly vanished. As it turned out, the sex scenes required little more than a simple shorthand, affording only the sparest of details. For example:

SEX SEQUENCE: ACTOR & ACTRESS, SS#1, B/G

It was my responsibility as a writer only to decide how many actors would participate, their exact gender, and the scene's sequential order in relation to the rest of the film. Simple as that. I might as well have been writing binary code, and that was exactly the way I liked it. It was hands-off erotica, leaving the dirty work to the professionals. I felt like a comedian who'd been hired only to create a joke's set-up, without having to bother with the exhausting chore of delivering a punchline.

It may seem that the writer is completely left out of the creative process, but some important decisions still had to be made. Would a particular scene involve just one man and one woman? Or should it get more risqué, with a third person introduced to the mix? My mind boggled at the mathematical possibilities.

It was beginning to look like this would be an altogether effortless writing experience. If I were so inclined, I could probably have cranked out a finished script in less than an hour, with time to spare for a snack and a short nap. But I wasn't willing to make it quite so easy. My sense of dignity wouldn't allow for such obvious hackery. If I was going to write trash, I wanted it at least to be intelligent trash. An apparent contradiction, but I felt up to the challenge. My script would include hints of irony, the occasional cultural send-up, maybe a little understated satire for the observant porn viewer. How hard could it be?

Two weeks later, I finished my first draft. I wouldn't have stopped revising it even then, had my wife not reminded me of my own self-imposed deadline.

"It's twenty freaking pages!" she yelled one evening. "What the hell do you think you're writing, goddamn *Beowulf*?"

I wouldn't have gone quite that far, but I was surprisingly proud. After a few finishing touches, I printed out my script and carefully placed it in a manila envelope. Tim had given me the name of the director he'd worked with, assuring me that unsolicited scripts were not only encouraged but industry policy. I checked and double-checked the address, terrified that my script might fall into the wrong hands. One wrong number on the zip code, and I was certain that some powerful movie exec would end up receiving my filthy prose. He would quickly spread the word around town that I was dabbling in the smut trade and should be avoided at all costs. My Hollywood career would be snuffed out as quickly as it had begun.

When a few weeks passed and I didn't hear back from the director, I could only assume the worst. I'd spent enough years in the writing trade to understand what prolonged silence meant. He had hated my script, if he'd read it at all. More than likely, it was still buried under a pile of submissions, lost in the shuffle like so many of my other literary efforts.

I wasn't offended. In fact, I was more than a little relieved, having come dangerously close to making a huge mistake. What had I been thinking anyway? Did I really believe that one measly paycheck would be worth the industry Scarlet Letter? I'd dodged a bullet, and should be thankful to have come out in one piece.

When I'd finally managed to forget the whole seedy affair, I received a phone call from a porn director named Brandon.

"Sorry it's taken me so long to get back to you," he said. "I just got around to reading your script. It was brilliant. Funny, funny stuff."

"Wow," I said, struggling not to appear unnerved by his kind words. "Thank you. I–"

"Of course, funny doesn't matter."

"Oh, well–"

"This is porn, right?" he said, a trace of giddy malice in his voice. "Who watches porn for the dialogue? Am I right or what?"

He broke into crunchy laughter, and I joined him, despite the fact that I was pretty sure he was insulting me.

"But, seriously, I loved it. I get a lot of crap scripts on my desk, but you managed to write something very special. It moved me, it really did."

I felt oddly gratified by his flattery. Sincere or not, he was hitting all the right buttons. True, I firmly believed that I'd written something better than average. But *moving*? I couldn't tell if he was just yanking my chain, or if I actually had an innate talent for churning out porn plots that managed to be both erotic and emotionally revealing.

"That was the easy part," Brandon went on. "Now you have to watch your beloved words get butchered by a bunch of high school drop-outs who wouldn't know a nice piece of prose if it up and bit them on the ass."

"Well, I'm sure–"

"I just want to prepare you, sport. I know how difficult this process can be. You think the actors are going to bring your vision to life, but then they rip out your heart and spit it back in your face."

I could only whimper in response.

"I mean, I love them and everything. Don't get me wrong. They're my people. Without them, I'm nothing. But come on, we all know that they're just shaved apes. You can't expect a miracle of evolution to happen overnight. You see what I'm saying?"

I didn't, but there was no point in telling him. I had to give this guy credit. His ability to build up a writer's ego and then bring it crashing down in a matter of seconds was simply awe-inspiring. I wasn't sure anymore if I was a genius with the potential to revolutionize an unfairly maligned industry, or just another cog in the oily, malfunctioning porn machine.

If my conflicting emotions were at all transparent, Brandon showed no sign of detecting them. "There's a lot of excitement around here about your script," he continued. "We're putting this project on the fast track."

"That's great."

"I just have to call the actors and crew. I'm guessing we'll be ready by Tuesday."

"Tuesday to start production?"

"No," he said. "Tuesday to shoot it."

"The whole thing?"

"Well, yeah." There was a brief moment of tense silence, and then Brandon began to laugh again. "You're serious, aren't you? I'm sorry, I forgot you were a newbie. Forgive me. Listen, why don't you come down to our offices tomorrow morning?

It'll give us a chance to meet face-to-face. And I'll be happy to answer all your questions."

"Actually, I'm not sure if—"

"Fantastic! I'll see you then."

I tried to protest, but Brandon was already gone. I remained on the phone, listening to the dial tone and finding an eerie significance in how much it sounded like a flatlining heartbeat.

I didn't sleep very well that night. Nightmares would rouse me from slumber every few hours. Most of them faded quickly from memory, but there was one dream that was so disturbing, it continues to haunt me to this day.

I'm one of the guests on the David Letterman show. He introduces me to the studio audience, and I'm greeted with wild cheers of adulation. I'm not sure what has made me such a popular figure in the mainstream, but I'm clearly a household name at this point. Dave shakes my hand and tells me how much my work has meant to him personally, a sentiment he seems to share with the rest of America. We joke good-naturedly about my latest projects, and I easily charm him with witty observations about the creative process and the hardships of being a literary giant in an era of low expectations.

When we've exhausted every minute detail about my incredible and multi-faceted career, Dave asks me about my long road to stardom.

"Well, it's funny you should bring that up, Dave," I tell him, winking at the audience. "Most people don't know this, but before I got my start in show business, I used to write porn films."

The silence is so abrupt, it's as if the laughter and applause were part of a pre-recorded loop that'd been switched off at the source. Dave stares at me with a baffled expression, not certain if this was some lame attempt at a comedy bit or if I had actually said what he thought I said.

"It was just one script," I say, the lack of confidence showing in my voice. "I was young and needed the money. But you can rest assured that I never–"

"Okay then," Dave says, cutting me off. "As much as we'd like to hear all about it, I'm afraid we've run out of time."

Dave cues his producers to cut to a commercial, and I know that it's over for me. The studio audience continues to gawk with a combination of fear and hatred in their eyes. A few of them even start to boo.

"It's not like I *still* do porn," I say, beginning to panic. "That was just a small part of my career. A very, very small part. Barely worth mentioning. I'm not even sure why I brought it up."

"Goodnight, everybody," Dave says, waving at the audience that has now risen to their feet and is howling for my blood. As Paul and the band begin to play, some burly stagehands walk onto the stage and grab me, roughly pulling me off the couch.

"Jerry Stahl did porno!" I scream at the audience as I'm dragged backstage. "You forgave him! Why can't you forgive me?"

As the stagehands throw me to the ground, I can see Stahl standing on the sidelines, glaring down at me. "Will you shut up about that?" he spits out, in a hushed tone more frightened than angry.

That's when I woke up, covered in sweat and trembling violently. I must have been screaming at some point, because my wife was awake when I came to my senses. She cradled me in her arms and gently stroked my hair until I drifted back to sleep.

"It was just a dream," she said. "You're safe now. Don't worry."

As much as I wanted to believe her, I knew that there was plenty to worry about.

2

Although I'd tried to acclimate to L.A. culture, I'd not yet bought into the local custom of loathing and generally avoiding the San Fernando Valley. But on this balmy morning in late July, it was the last place on earth that I wanted to be.

As I drove through the streets of Canoga Park, searching for the offices of my future employers, I could begin to understand why the Valley had earned its maligned reputation. It's less a suburban oasis than an apocalyptic dustbowl, an unfathomably ugly sprawl of strip malls, factories and cul-de-sacs. The affordable housing and lower crime rate hardly make it any more attractive. Despite its good intentions, it can only ever hope to be L.A.'s ugly sister to the north, the last stop for Hollywood failures and ne'er-do-wells, a rarely visited graveyard where celebrity pool cleaners go to die.

And the heat must only be experienced to be truly believed. The Santa Monica mountains, which form the Valley's southern boundary, manage to shield it from the refreshing coastal breezes that cool the rest of Los Angeles. During the summer months, the Valley is always at least ten degrees hotter, and exponentially more humid, than anywhere else in Southern California. From the moment you cross the border, it feels like you've ventured inside the mouth of a dog.

On the surface, you'd never know that this seemingly working-class neighborhood was actually the self-appointed capital of porn. Over three-fourths of the adult films produced in the free world come from the Valley, and more production companies are moving there every day. Which brings up an obvious question: What could they possibly be thinking? Despite the sunny climate and close proximity to an endless pool of frustrated young starlets with dreams bigger than their talents, there doesn't seem to be any good reason why anyone in any entertainment field would willingly call this unwashed armpit of the universe their home.

Probably the only good reason why porn continues to thrive in this region is because it would be unwelcome anywhere else. The porn industry and the Valley have developed an unspoken symbiotic relationship that neither would ever openly admit. The Valley's middle-class community, founded with the slogan "The Town That Started Right," saw itself evolve into "The Valley of Sin" without putting up so much as a snivel in protest.

And why would they? For most of its existence, the Valley was little more than a working class refuge and a cheap source of water for L.A. But since porn producers began setting up shop on their turf, it has transformed into the epicenter of a flourishing, billion dollar industry. While the production of feature films in Los Angeles has decreased almost 13% over the past decade, adult movie production is up 25% and rising.

Americans regularly spend more than eight billion dollars a year on hardcore videos, an amount easily three times larger than all of Hollywood's domestic box office receipts.

And that translates to rising employment. Porn productions annually bring as many as 20,000 new jobs to the Valley. And those numbers don't just include the uninhibited men and women having sex in front of the camera. Pornos also hire cameramen, gaffers, grips, and sound engineers. That's a lot of checks being written, which results in more homes being built in the area and more money being spent on local businesses. Even the most porn- loathing Valley native must appreciate that the math works out in their favor.

Perhaps in reciprocation towards the Valley's open-door policy towards porn, producers have taken great strides not to flaunt their dirty secrets in public. While Hollywood's studios advertise their presence with glitzy overkill, porn studios are downright inconspicuous, if not totally invisible. There are almost three hundred porn facilities within the Valley limits — including sound stages, editing facilities, and printing plants — but they're hidden with such expertise that even their own neighbors couldn't identify them with any certainty. On a daily basis, an empire of porn is created without anybody knowing the better.

Everybody gets rich. Everybody is happy. And it all happens behind closed doors, keeping the illusion of a moral community fabric alive and well.

As much as I could appreciate the beauty of this system, I couldn't help but be a little annoyed by how it had personally inconvenienced me. It's all well and good that the locals don't have to be constantly reminded of their porn surroundings, but for an outsider like myself, it made finding a correct address an impossible challenge. Forget a map, I needed a compass. It's not like I wanted a big flashing neon sign that screamed PORN STUDIO, but it wouldn't have killed them to put a few numbers on the doors.

Using the process of elimination, I eventually found my way to the right building. Hidden behind a fence of shrubbery on a quiet residential street, it barely qualified as an inhabitable place of business. There were no windows, barbed-wire fences surrounded all corners, and all but one of the doors was locked with a padlock. The elaborate security measures were probably intended to scare away horny teenagers and curious tourists, but I couldn't shake the feeling that I was trespassing on a hostile religious compound.

I finally managed to find an unlocked door, and entered into what appeared to be a rather ordinary reception area. It was clean and well lit, reminiscent of a dentist's office. Not exactly the strip club atmosphere I'd been anticipating. But I was immediately reminded of who owned these premises when I was greeted by a big-breasted secretary, dressed in a low-cut dress that revealed far more cleavage than I was ready to witness so early in the morning.

"Hello," she said brightly, smiling up at me. "Are you here for the gang-bang auditions?"

"Uh, no," I said. "I have an appointment with Brandon Holly. I'm a writer."

Her smile vanished. "Okay then," she said coldly. "Have a seat and I'll let him know you're here."

I wandered over to a couch in the far corner of the room. As I flipped though the magazines laid out on a small coffee table (which included, strangely enough, copies of *Consumer Reports* and *Psychology Today*), I wondered exactly what was involved in a gang-bang audition. Was a headshot and resumé required? Would you be asked to prepare a monologue? Probably best not to give it too much thought. That way madness lies.

"Is that Spitznagel?" a voice boomed. I looked up and saw a thin man coming towards me, his hand outstretched in greeting.

"Glad you could make it, sport," he said, practically pulling me to my feet with his grip. "I'm Brandon. Welcome to our happy little home."

Though he seemed to be in his late thirties, there was something about him that reminded me of a teenage girl with bulimia. The skin was stretched so tightly across his face that when he smiled, his cheekbones threatened to crumble and break like old taffy. And his ribcage was frighteningly transparent through his loose satin shirt. This was a man in desperate need of nourishment.

"Let's find someplace more private," he said, winking at me.

I followed him through a maze of hallways, designed to make escape impossible. We eventually entered a conference room, its walls lined with the boxes of their more popular videos. It was unsettling to be surrounded by so many pictures of naked models. I had the weird sensation that the eyes were following me, leering with forced, insincere lust.

We both found a chair on either side of a large table.

"Can I get you some coffee?" Brandon offered. I shook my head, not sure if my immune system could withstand the hot liquid syphilis that undoubtedly passed for coffee at this place.

"Let's get down to business," he said. "I love your script. Went ballistic over it. Wouldn't change a thing."

"Thank you," I said.

"That said, I had to make a few changes."

"Oh, okay."

"Nothing major," he said. "I just cut some of the more complicated words."

"I'm not sure what you mean."

"It's okay, you didn't know. But for future reference, try to stay away from words with more than three syllables. It just frustrates the actors and they can't perform. And when they can't perform, we don't get paid. You see what I'm saying, sport?"

The way he kept calling me "sport" sent a chill down my spine. It made him sound like a dirty old uncle, drunk at a holiday family gathering, trying to coax an underage nephew into sitting on his lap.

"So," he said, slapping a hand on my knee. "What else have you got for me?"

I just stared back at him, not entirely sure what he wanted. "I'm sorry?"

"What are you working on now? Anything new and exciting?"

"You mean... scripts?"

"Hell yes, I mean scripts. What'd you think, this was just a friendly get-together? I want to hear some ideas! I want to crawl into that head of yours and mine it for gold! I want to suckle at your creative teat!"

To say that I was caught off-guard would have been a gross understatement. Never suspecting that I'd been invited to a pitch session, I was completely unprepared for such a possibility. Maybe I could have improvised a few ideas for him, had I not been so deeply troubled by what my "creative teat" might be, and why this strange, skinny man was so eager to suckle at it.

Brandon must have seen the panic in my face, because he quickly filled the silence. "I have an idea that I've been tossing around," he said. "I've just been waiting for the right writer to give it to, and I think you're my man. Are you ready for it?"

"Sure," I said tentatively.

He paused for a moment, letting the tension build in what he hoped was a hushed awe. And then, letting the word leave his lips softly as a whisper, he said, "Kurosawa."

I just stared back at him. If this was his idea, obviously I'd missed something. "You mean the filmmaker?" I asked.

"Have you ever watched one of Kurosawa's films and thought, 'Damn, this would've made a great porno'?"

Honestly, the thought had never crossed my mind. Not once. But that didn't stop me from nodding excitedly at Brandon, as if he had hit upon some universal truth. "Well, sure," I replied. "Who hasn't?"

My enthusiasm just seemed to incite him, and he leaned closer. "I've always wondered what *Rashomon* would have been like as an adult film. Different versions of events, multiple points of view, a cinematic meditation on the subjective nature of truth. Add some fucking, and it practically writes itself."

He was a madman, that much was clear. But I felt compelled to ride this runaway train off the tracks and hold on until the last possible second. "I think you may be onto something," I said.

"This is my vision, Eric," he said. "I need you to give it life."

"Well, I–"

"I'm not saying it's going to be easy. The boys in finance don't want this. They're calling for your head. They think you're trying to ruin the company."

"Wait, I didn't–"

"But I'm going to fight for you. I believe in you and I believe in your idea. Ask anybody, I take care of my people. If I stand for nothing else, it's protecting my talent."

The joke had gone too far, and it was time to make a jump for safety. I glanced at my watch, attempting to look surprised, as if I had only just realized that I was late for another appointment.

"I'd better be going," I said. "I'll be in touch though, okay?" He seemed to buy it, which was enough for now. As long as I could get out of there without promising anything, I would be safe. I made a mental note to have my phone number changed the moment I got home.

I was standing up to leave when the door to the conference room suddenly slammed open and a short, pudgy man entered the room.

"Hey, Brandon," the man said. "You almost done here? I've only got the soundstage reserved until noon."

He was dressed in an old t-shirt and jeans, stained with splashes of dried paint and plaster. His chin was covered in coarse stubble, and judging from his ripe odor and oily hair, it'd been days since his last shower.

"Ian, great, there's someone I want you to meet." Brandon turned to me, placing an arm around my shoulder. "This is Eric, one of our newest writers."

"Hello," I said, forcing a smile.

Ian just glared at me, his nostrils flaring. He nodded in greeting but made no attempt to conceal his immediate contempt. I felt quite certain that if Brandon wasn't standing nearby, he might have taken a swing at me.

"You'll have to pardon Ian's appearance," Brandon said, ignoring the palpable tension in the room. "He's been up all night putting the finishing touches on one of our sets."

"Oh, that's great," I said.

"He's also an actor," Brandon continued. "And when he has time, he's a cinematographer, editor and executive producer."

I could fathom this man as a carpenter, and possibly even a producer, but picturing him as an actor seemed like a bit of a stretch. His sizable paunch and questionable hygiene made it inconceivable that anybody, anywhere, would want to see him naked.

"Well, it was nice to meet you," I said.

Ian's eyes narrowed in evident disdain, and he turned his gaze back to Brandon. "Just make it quick, okay?"

With that, he turned and left, and I released a heavy sigh of relief. Brandon chuckled under his breath, apparently delighted by Ian's reaction. "I hope you didn't take any of that personally, sport," he said. "Ian just doesn't like outsiders."

"I see."

"Nobody around here does. They just assume that because you're new, you can't be trusted. Give them some time and they'll learn to accept you."

Fat chance of that, I thought. I had no intention of sticking around this place any longer than necessary. If they didn't like me now, I'll just have to live without their approval.

"So," Brandon said, blocking the door with his gaunt frame. "Do we have a deal?"

"Sorry?"

"Are you writing my script or what?"

I'm not sure what I was thinking. I knew that the smart move would have been to politely decline his offer. But I said yes, I'd write his script. And worse still, I *meant* it.

I suppose I just couldn't back away from a challenge. Brandon's earnest, if misguided, belief in my abilities as a writer was difficult to resist. I certainly wasn't deluded enough to think I could create a porno script with any degree of artistic significance. I was not about to buy into that cliché, which had plagued the porno industry long before I'd entered the game. Films like *Behind the Green Door* and *Café Flesh* notwithstanding, porn has never succeeded in rising above its filthy roots. On those rare occasions when porn auteurs have attempted to reach beyond their creative grasp, making films with ambitions of dramatic credibility, it's almost always resulted in a humiliating self-parody. There are already enough reasons to laugh at porn, but when it aspires towards something more than its assigned cultural niche, it only confirms the long-standing belief that art should be left to the artists.

But what if I could find a way to bring porno into the mainstream through the back door? What if I wrote a script that was so funny, so original, so utterly campy that no amount of bad acting or poor production values could ruin it?

It wouldn't happen overnight. At first, just a few observant viewers would notice the change. They'd begin actually paying attention to the plot without hovering a thumb over the remote's fast forward button. Eventually, they would invite their friends for late-night screenings, and together they'd howl over their favorite lines. Before long, midnight shows of my porno would become the latest rage among young urban hipsters, and fans would show up dressed as their favorite character. It would evolve into an international craze, and soon even the critics would come around, admitting that my porno, though by no means culturally relevant, at least qualified as a fairly decent guilty pleasure.

It was the difference between being Ed Wood or John Waters. If porn was destined to be a joke, then so be it. But I wanted to be *in* on the joke.

These were the fantasies that danced through my head as I drove home on the Ronald Reagan Expressway. How wonderfully ironic, I thought, that the one highway leading in and out of the center of Porn-ville would be named after the very president who sought to destroy it. And irony was, after all, exactly what I hoped to bring back to the porno industry.

I was well aware that my new benefactors probably wouldn't fall to my will quite so easily. There would be the obvious misgivings. But irony, I would remind them, is a word with only three syllables, and that should be enough to appease them.

Quite honestly, I didn't care if they understood what I was trying to do. I would simply deliver the scripts, and let nature run its course. So long as they spoke the lines that I gave them, and followed my outlines to the letter, the rest of the plan would take care of itself. It was simply a matter of working with their shortcomings, using their flaws to my advantage. They were clay, ready to be molded into whatever shape I saw fit.

Before returning to our apartment, I stopped at a local video store to peruse their porn selection. Some research on the competition was necessary, if only to see how my contemporaries had tried and failed. I picked six or seven titles at random and brought them to the register.

"This isn't what you think," I told the store's sole employee as he scanned my videos. "I'm just doing a study of current trends in adult erotica."

The employee just shrugged. "Whatever you say."

"Pretty soon you won't need that," I said, pointing to the partition that separated the porn section from the rest of the store. "I'm going to make an adult video that won't have to be kept in a back room, hidden away like some kind of cinematic embarrassment."

He pushed the videos across the counter and asked, "Do you want a bag with that?"

"No, thank you," I said, picking up my bounty. "I'm not ashamed of renting porn. I'm going to walk out of here with my head held high."

And I did just that. At least until I left the store. When the warm rays of the afternoon sun fell upon me, I had a sudden surge of paranoia. Cradling the videos close to my chest, I scurried towards my car like a frightened cockroach exposed by the sudden flip of a kitchen light switch.

3

The phone started ringing around 5 a.m. I tried to ignore it, waiting for the answering machine to pick up. But whoever was calling didn't bother to leave a message, and they called back a few seconds later. When that failed, the phone rang again. And again.

I put a pillow over my head, praying they'd give up eventually. But the ringing didn't stop, and soon it seemed that my head might explode from the throbbing. My wife groaned in protest, prodding me with a sleepy hand.

Crawling out of bed, I reached for the phone. "Hello?"

"Good morning, sunshine," a gruff voice answered.

"Who is this?"

"Your new best fucking friend."

He told me that his name was Raymond, and he directed videos for a major porn studio that I recognized instantly, even with my limited knowledge of the industry.

"Brandon showed me that script you wrote for him," Ray said. "Fucking funny. It cracked me up. Nearly shit my pants."

Although I always enjoy unsolicited compliments, it was a tad jarring to be roused from slumber with the news that my prose had somehow inspired incontinence in a complete stranger.

"I want you to write for us," he said.

I closed the door to our bedroom and walked out into the hall. "Wow," I said. "I don't know what to say."

"Say 'Yes'."

"I'd love to, I really would. But I already promised to write another script for Brandon."

Ray sighed, but it seemed that he'd been expecting this. "Let me guess," he said. "He gave you the Kurosawa pitch, didn't he?"

"Yeah, how did you—?"

"He's been talking that same bullshit for years. It's just a mid-life crisis. Poor bastard is worried about his legacy."

"Oh... well—"

"Forget about it. Come work for us. The money's better, and we won't ask you to write like some obscure Chinese filmmaker."

I considered mentioning that Kurosawa was neither obscure nor Chinese, but decided against it. I was intrigued by his offer. I'd been struggling with the *Rashomon* script for days, and kept running up against the same creative hurdles, the most glaring being that the idea was just inherently stupid. Here was my chance to ditch a losing prospect and start fresh.

Luckily, I'd been preparing for just such an opportunity. "I have a few of my own ideas," I said. "If you'd like to hear them, I could—"

"Forget it," Ray interrupted. "I have a project that I think would be perfect for you. It's called *Butt Crazy*."

"O-okay."

"Volume thirteen."

"It's a sequel?"

"It's not just a sequel," he insisted. "It's the most popular series our company puts out. I'm taking a big chance on you. This is our most lucrative franchise, and I'm putting it in your hands."

I suppose it's telling that my first reaction wasn't utter horror at the prospect of writing a script with the title *Butt Crazy*. My main concern was that it was a sequel. Not that I'd even seen any of the other films, but a sequel seemed a little redundant. Was there really anything left to say on the subject of butts or butt-related insanity that hadn't been *explored ad nauseum* in the first twelve films? It was well-trodden ground not befitting an artist of my stature.

On the other hand, it was a major production at a major porn studio. I might have liked to develop an original script, but this route could mean a lot less headaches. There would be no pitch sessions, no struggling for creative control, no nervous memos from financial backers. It was a pre-sold project with proven profit potential. With the high stakes involved, they weren't likely to skimp. I could reasonably expect a bigger budget, a salary hike, and possibly even my own trailer on the set. The expectations would be high, but I felt up to the task. Yes, I told myself, I would be a fool to pass up this opportunity.

"Count me in," I said. "Will I be working off an outline?"

"Excuse me?" Ray asked.

"What's the story about?"

"What story?"

"For the movie."

Ray said nothing, but I could almost hear his face tighten in agitation. "What the fuck are you talking about?" he growled. "Who said anything about a story?"

"Isn't there a plot?" I asked.

"It's *Butt Crazy*," he said, as if I'd missed an obvious clue. "It's about fucking butts."

"Yes, but–"

"Listen, I love your writing. You've got a keen eye for dialogue. But you're making this more complicated than it needs to be."

"Okay," I sighed.

"Just get me twenty pages by next Tuesday."

"And make it about... butts?"

"That's right. Bunch of girls with sexy butts. Give them something funny to say, and we're in business."

I knew better than to continue this line of discussion. For whatever reason, I'd pushed the limits of his patience. But I needed more information if I was going to make this work. "Now when you say 'something funny,' you mean what exactly?"

"Just fucking funny. What else do you want?"

"So you don't want them saying anything specific?"

"Listen to me," he screamed. "Shut the fuck up and listen. It's about *butts*. Write me a script about *butts*."

"Gotcha," I said, miserably. "No problem."

"Are you gonna be able to handle this, or do I have to find another writer?"

"No, no, I can do it," I assured him. "Butts. Funny. Twenty pages. Couldn't be clearer."

"Alright, I'll call you on Monday."

"Should I–?"

"I said *I'll* call *you*! Jesus Christ, fucking writers."

The phone went dead, and I placed it back on the receiver. I staggered back into the bedroom and crawled under the covers. Maybe it was just a bad dream, I told myself. I'll wake up in a few hours and realize that the phone call never happened. But I knew I was just fooling myself.

"Who was that?" my wife asked groggily.

"You don't want to know," I said, before drifting back to sleep.

Over the next week, I felt strangely optimistic. I still hadn't heard from my agent, but I didn't much care anymore. I had not one but *two* directors practically begging me to write for them. That the films they made were outlawed in most of Middle America, and even considered a felony in states like Utah and Florida, seemed an irrelevant detail. I had finally been accepted by Hollywood, or at least Hollywood's addled half-sister who lived down in the basement.

When I wasn't writing, I spent my free time watching hundreds of adult videos. After the initial shock wore off, it became a mindless chore lacking any of the erotic delights I had once enjoyed during my youth. It's quite a different experience to watch porn with an eye towards story deconstruction. There were times when I completely lost track of my remote. And on more than one occasion, I would fast forward through the sex to get back to the dialogue. My porn research became such a standard routine, I thought nothing of screening a few videos with lunch, a habit my wife quickly banned, claiming it was "disgusting."

It'd been years since I'd rented porn with any regularity, so I had no idea what to expect. I was surprised at how few films contained anything that even remotely resembled a plot. Most relied on the *cinema-vérité* style known as "Gonzo," which basically entailed pointing a camera at the actors and letting them improvise. It had all the narrative power of a home movie, with none of the context.

After watching countless hours of these videos, my task suddenly took on a larger sense of importance. At least within the realm of porn, the sanctity of storytelling itself was in jeopardy. I was a holy troubadour on a crusade to save the industry not just from lazy filmmaking but from total artistic irrelevance.

My head filled with lofty ideals, I began calling friends — friends I hadn't spoken to in years — and announced my porn ambitions without shame. I expected them to be horrified but they were surprisingly supportive, even encouraging. Stranger still, more than a few of my writer friends admitted that they too had dabbled in porn from time to time, if only to pay the bills while they waited for more substantial work to come along.

I began to suspect that I was involved in something far more universal than I'd originally believed. By agreeing to write porn, I had started down a path that'd become a modern rite of passage among aspiring scribes. While writers from past generations had cut their teeth writing short stories for pulp magazines, today's young and unknown authors were beginning their careers in the smut trade.

Inspired by their approval, I decided to take a chance. I called the one person least likely to understand just what the hell I was thinking. Despite all common sense, I called my mother.

Mom had never approved of my moving to L.A. in the first place. She was concerned that the smog would irritate my asthma. Never mind the fact that I didn't have — nor had I ever had —

asthma. Perhaps she just wanted to scare me away from a losing prospect. My forays into journalism, with its feast-or-famine paydays, had made her more than nervous but the thought of her son as a struggling screenwriter was enough to keep her up at nights. The odds were against me, she'd say. I'd have a better chance of winning the lottery (which, to her credit, was not far from the truth). As far as she was concerned, the only responsible career choice for a writer was to become a teacher. That I had no interest in becoming a full-time academic continued to confound and annoy her.

"Have you lost your mind?" was her response when I told her the news.

"Now hear me out," I pleaded.

"What could you possibly say that would make this less of a catastrophe?"

"You're overreacting."

"I told you that L.A. would be the ruin of you," she wailed, near tears. "Didn't I say that?"

"It's just one script, Mom. Nobody will ever know I did it."

"That's what you think. It starts with the writing, and the next thing you know, you're taking off your clothes for the camera."

"Do you know how silly that sounds?"

"It's not silly at all. People get tricked into appearing in porn every day. Don't be so confident that it won't happen to you."

I wanted to assure her that she had nothing to worry about. There was one very good reason why I would never appear in a porn movie. But there's just no tactful way of telling your mother that you have a small penis.

"These porn people can't be trusted," she warned me.

"They'll get you hopped up on drugs so you don't know what you're doing."

"That's not true," I countered.

"Oh, isn't it? I saw a report on *60 Minutes*. A bunch of pimps and junkies, that's what they are."

"You're going to have to trust me on this. I know what I'm doing."

"You'll end up like that Marilyn Chambers girl. She had a wonderful career doing Ivory Soap commercials, and then she threw it all away."

Resistance was futile. I could argue with her all day but she'd always have another fact in her arsenal, another nugget of information to validate her fears. She had done her homework and there was nothing I could do or say to change her mind.

"Father," she said, "will you please tell him that this isn't a good idea?"

My dad had been mostly silent during our conversation. I was sure he didn't share my mom's paranoia, but he had to be at least a little disappointed. He always enjoyed bragging about my books and magazine stories to anybody willing to listen. He even took an unblushing pride when I started writing for *Playboy*. All the same, I didn't think he could find a way to spin this. I found it hard to imagine him strolling into work, carrying a box filled with videotapes. "Step right up, folks," he'd say. "Get your free copy of *Anal Way You Like It*. My son wrote it, y'know."

My father clicked his tongue nervously which usually indicated that he was having trouble finding the diplomatic middle road. "Well," he said finally, "I understand your mother's concerns."

"You see?" my mother howled. "We both think you're being foolish!"

"But," he interrupted, "we might want to look for the bright side in all this."

Clearly my father was going to be the voice of reason. He would remind my mom that though she didn't approve of my methods, I would at least be bringing home a paycheck. It was in their best interests, as it meant I wouldn't be calling them for another loan. How could they not be pleased that I was finally on the road to financial self-sufficiency?

But perhaps that was too obvious. My father opted instead for a different tack, one that none of us saw coming.

"Our boy is going to be in the Vatican," he announced.

It took me a moment to realize what he meant. According to an old urban legend, the Vatican Library contains the largest collection of pornography in the world. Although nobody has ever seen it, the basement is supposedly filled with millions of porn reels, videos, and erotic antiquities spanning from the Roman Empire to present day. It seemed unlikely that there was any truth to the stories but I wasn't going to be the one to bring that up.

"Are you drunk?" my mom asked.

There was no dissuading my father once he had an idea in his head. "I think it's kinda neat," he continued. "Something you've written will be stored just a few floors below the Pope."

I couldn't believe my good fortune. Whether he knew it or not, my father had jumped on a live grenade for me. It was such a sweet gesture, I couldn't let him go down alone.

"You think he ever gets lonely and goes downstairs to take a peek?" I wondered aloud.

My father giggled. "Probably."

"Oh, for goodness sakes," my mother exclaimed. But she knew when she was outnumbered. The battle was over, and I had somehow come out unscathed.

I finished the first draft of *Butt Crazy* in only two hours. To this day, I couldn't tell you what it was about. All evidence of it seems to have disappeared, and judging from my hazy recollections, that's probably for the best.

A few days after I delivered the script to Ray, he called me at home. He was not happy.

"I-I don't even know where to begin," he sputtered, so livid that he could barely speak. "This is awful. Completely unusable. I don't know if this is your idea of a joke, but it isn't fucking funny."

"What's wrong with it?"

"For starters, everybody's fucking talking. Every page, there's talking, talking, talking. I couldn't even finish the damn thing, it gave me a fucking headache."

I could hear distant voices grumbling behind him. They seemed to be cursing. I'm not sure if their rage was directed at me, but I didn't feel inclined to ask.

"I thought that's what you wanted," I said.

"Well, you thought wrong. You've got a monologue on page seven that's almost *three* lines long."

"It wasn't supposed to be a monologue. I–"

He must have started slamming the phone's receiver against a wall, because for the next few seconds, all I could hear were sharp banging sounds.

"Listen to me," he snarled. "Just shut up for one goddamn minute and listen to me. Do you know what you're asking? You're asking me to find a cast that can memorize lines *and* perform on cue. Do you have any concept of what a rarity that is in this industry?"

"I don't–"

"You ever see a porn actor try to speak in complete sentences? Their fucking synapses catch on fire."

"I'm sorry. Let me try again. I promise the second draft will be better."

"Don't bother," he said, his fury disappearing as quickly as it came. "We're going with a different direction."

He told me that the company had just been offered use of a 24-room estate in the Malibu hills. "Get a pen," he said. "I want you to write this down. It's got a master bedroom, a lighthouse, a tennis court, two pools, and a gazebo."

I did as he asked, though I wasn't sure what he expected me to do with this information.

"You're always whining about needing an outline," he said. "I decided to give you one this time."

By no means did I consider myself an expert in screenplay technique, but I was fairly sure that what he'd just given me wasn't a typical three-act story structure. "No problem," I said, though I couldn't have had less of an idea what he wanted from me.

"Oh, and one more thing," he added. "Our lead actress is from Stockholm and she has a really cool accent, so try to work that into the script."

"O-okay."

"And she has a prosthetic leg."

"Sorry?"

"It's made of wood, I think. And the fucking thing is detachable. Wait till you see it. It'll blow your fucking mind. She's a little shy but if we're lucky, we might be able to get her to do a few scenes without the leg."

A mental image flashed through my mind but it was too

horrible, I had to squash it out. I scribbled the words "German Cripple" in my notes, and left it at that.

"Great," I said. "I'll get right on it."

"Get me a first draft by tomorrow."

"One question. Do you still want it to be about butts?"

"Of course I want it to be about butts," he snarled. "This is porno. They're *all* about butts."

"I just thought–"

"Well, stop it. I'm paying you to write, not to second-guess me. Just get it done."

"Okay," I said.

"And get it right this time, will you? I want to look at the first page and see lots of empty, white spaces."

Ray hung up almost before he'd finished speaking. Moments later, my phone was ringing again. I picked it up.

"Spitz, baby," a cheery voice greeted me. "It's Brandon."

The panic washed over me like a wave. I'd promised to finish his Kurosawa script within the week and I hadn't bothered to tell him that I'd given up on the project.

"Oh, hi," I stammered. "How's it going?"

"Fine," he said. "Are you okay? You sound nervous."

"No, no, it's nothing. I just... So, what's happening?"

I really had no reason to feel guilty. It's not like I'd signed a contract or had any sense of loyalty towards this man. But I'd given him my word, and then I went behind his back and made alliances with one of his competitors. There's nothing quite so humbling as realizing that you've acted more cowardly than a porn director.

"Listen, I need to tell you something," I said urgently.

"Save it," he replied. "I haven't heard from you in a while, and I just wanted to call and tell you that we're shooting your script tomorrow."

My jaw almost dropped to the floor. I suppose that I hadn't really believed it would get this far. To have a script actually go into production — be it porn or otherwise — was like some beautiful dream. It was the kind of thing that only happened to real screenwriters. I felt validated, as if all my hopes and aspirations might not be so far out of reach after all.

"So you want to come and watch?" he asked.

"Really? You wouldn't mind?"

"Not at all. We'd love to have you."

I'd long fantasized about visiting the set of my first movie. I envisioned it all, played out every detail. I saw myself sitting silently in the shadows, in a chair with my name embroidered on the back in bold letters. The director would occasionally call me over to advise on how a certain scene should be played. Even the actors would not be able to resist pulling me aside to request some insight on what a particular passage had meant, or to debate the underlying themes of my script. Although I had only come to watch, I'd feel compelled to rewrite entire pages of dialogue, which the actors would accept without complaint. The crew would agree that, of all the writers they'd worked with, none had demonstrated such an awe-inspiring standard of excellence, not to mention a stunning ability to create art on the spot.

This was my dream, and I wanted it so badly, I could taste it.

Brandon dictated directions to the studio, and advised me not to show up until at least after noon. "That's when the real action happens," he said.

It wasn't until hours later that I realized what Brandon had meant by "action." I wouldn't just be watching actors speak my words. I would also be watching sex. Actual flesh and blood humans engaging in carnal hydraulics right in front of me. It was quite the moral quandary. Writing for these smut fiends was easily justifiable, if only because I could keep a safe distance from their world. But visiting the set would be crossing a line. I would be right inside the belly of the beast where the distinction between porn professional and casual participant wasn't quite so clear anymore.

I considered calling Brandon and telling him that I wouldn't be able to make it. But I didn't. I wanted that chair with my name embroidered on the back, goddammit. And if surrounding myself with naked, beautiful women was the only way to get it, well, that was a price I was willing to pay.

4

"I'm here to see Brandon," I said.

A bald man with heavily tattooed arms peered at me with bored indifference. He seemed uncertain whether to let me pass or give me a thorough pummeling.

"I'm a writer," I said. "They're shooting my script today. Brandon told me to meet him here."

The man continued to stare, saying nothing. He leaned back in his chair and rested his feet against the wall, creating a makeshift barricade.

It had taken all morning just to find this place. After wandering through an abandoned industrial zone in the Valley for what seemed like hours, I eventually found the studio, which was yet another building with no windows and no apparent street address. I had come too far to let some hired goon stand in my way now.

"Do you need to see an ID or something?" I asked. "Because

I really need to get in there. They're expecting me."

The man cracked a grin, amused by my desperation. He took a long draw from his cigarette and then gestured with his head towards a flight of stairs. I nodded at him in thanks and walked up the stairs, my legs trembling and threatening to give way at any moment.

Entering a dimly lit hallway, I was immediately enveloped in darkness. I waved my hands, searching for something to guide me. I found a cushioned wall and pressed my body against it. Following noises that sounded like rhythmic moaning, I hugged the wall like I might fall to my death if I let go even for a second.

As I crept down the hallway, it didn't appear that I was getting any closer to the end. The voices were getting louder but there wasn't even a glimmer of light in the distance. I began to panic, certain that I would never find my way out of this hellish abyss. And then, quite suddenly, the wall ended. I flailed wildly with my free hand, but all I could feel was air. The moaning seemed to be right next to me, but I was still blinded by darkness.

I staggered into the void and landed with a crash. Almost immediately, I felt the warm glow of light on my face.

"Cut!"

I looked up and saw that I was lying in the middle of a large room, built to resemble a hotel lobby. From every corner, strange men were staring down at me. Some held boom mikes or lighting equipment, others stood behind cameras. In the middle of the room, Brandon was sitting on an old leather couch. He was dressed in a bellhop uniform, complete with cap and tux jacket, except he wasn't wearing pants. Kneeling before him was a busty women, her hair so heavily bleached that it had turned white. She was completely naked and her face was buried in Brandon's lap.

"That was one hell of an entrance, sport," Brandon said, baring his teeth in greeting.

The crew sighed in unison, relieved that I was not an unexpected intruder. I said nothing, barely able to blink. Taking a nose-dive into the middle of a film set was bad enough, but to suddenly find myself on eye level with a blowjob in progress was mortifying on too many levels.

"Do me a favor and sit over there," Brandon said, pointing towards a couple of folding chairs behind the camera. "You're in our shot."

Although my extremities had gone numb, I somehow got to my feet and scurried out of the glaring floodlights.

"Okay, let's try it from the top," Brandon announced, adjusting himself while the actress took a much needed breather. I collapsed into a free chair, relieved to no longer be the center of attention. In the next seat was a greasy man wearing an old t-shirt and jeans, his limp brown hair highlighted with streaks of blonde. He was studying a monitor, which played back everything the camera was recording, and listening intently to a pair of headphones strapped to his head.

"Exciting work, huh?" I said, trying to be friendly.

He ignored me so I looked around the room for some other distraction. I pretended to be fascinated by a random crew member, busy changing a gel on one of the lighting fixtures.

"Roll camera," Brandon shouted.

"Rolling," the cameraman shouted back.

"And action," Brandon barked. His face contorted into an expression of pain or pleasure, I'm not sure which. The actress returned to her task with machine-like precision, making up in technical prowess what she lacked in enthusiasm.

Brandon's grinding hips caused the leather upholstery to squeak under his bare buttocks. The actress, as if waiting for just such an excuse, began to titter. Brandon rolled his eyes and shot a sidelong glance at the cameraman.

"We can fix it in editing," he said, waving at Brandon to continue.

"Oh, yeah, baby," Brandon groaned, effortlessly returning into character. "Oh yeah. Oh yeah. Do it. Uaaahuh. Whoaaah. Mmmmm yeah, mmmmm yeah. Here comes the room rate!"

I found some comfort in focusing on the monitor, as it gave me the illusion that the horrifying sexual act being performed just a few feet away was actually taking place somewhere else. The camera's lens zoomed in and out, searching for the perfect gynecological detail. Every shot seemed like a blur of random fleshy bits, bent in improbable angles that made it impossible to know for certain what it was you were looking at. A disembodied hand came into view, and just as quickly disappeared. I saw something that could have passed for either a nose or a testicle. I supposed this too would be "fixed in editing," though it would be a challenge with so little usable footage.

The muffled moans reached a fever pitch, and with that I had seen enough. I tried to force myself into a trance. It seemed like the only reasonable alternative to watching this gruesome union reach its inevitable conclusion. I let my mind wander, hoping eventually to tune out all the sights and sounds that threatened to drive me mad. But as my eyes drifted around the room, a haunting thought occurred.

I had not written a scene that in any way involved either a hotel lobby or a bellboy.

Turning to the monitor guy, who was adjusting a soundboard with delicate precision, I whispered, "Excuse me, you wouldn't happen to have a copy of the script, would you?"

Once again, he ignored me. But I saw a script on the floor next to him and grabbed it. I flipped through the pages, scanning for any mention of a hotel. There was none.

"Can I ask you a question?" I interrupted, tugging at the monitor guy's sleeve.

Reluctantly, the man turned and glared. "What?" he hissed.

"I'm a little confused. Are you shooting just one movie today?"

"Course."

"And what's the name of it again?"

He told me. It was the same title I'd given my script. Something was very wrong here.

"You're sure?" I asked. "The reason I'm asking is, I wrote it and I don't remember writing this particular scene."

His eyes widened in mock horror. "Dear God, no," he said. "Well, we better stop production right away. We can't finish this thing if the *story* isn't right."

He sniffed, and turned his gaze back towards the monitor.

"Alright, people, let's break for lunch," Brandon declared. The actress had already left the set and Brandon was wrapping himself in a towel.

"Thanks a lot, pal," the monitor guy snarled. "We missed all the good stuff."

I didn't even hear him. I was too busy re-reading my script, wondering what else had been changed.

Say what you will about the low production values in porn — they don't skimp when it comes to catering. An elaborate spread of fruits, pastries, and cold cuts were laid out for the cast and crew, and they took to it like vultures on a dead horse. Their plates piled high with comestibles, they crowded into booths and enjoyed a leisurely lunch that would last well into the afternoon.

I sat at an empty booth and picked at my food, trying to look preoccupied making notes in the script. Not that I expected to be welcomed with open arms, but a nod in my direction would have been nice. Some acknowledgment of my presence. But their complete disregard made it painfully clear that they wanted nothing to do with me.

As much as I pretended not to care, it really bothered me. It was one thing to stand at a safe distance and feel superior to the poor, pitiful rabble who make their living performing in pornos. It's quite another thing to be openly shunned by them. I couldn't fathom why these social misfits could afford to exclude anybody. And their rejection of me only made them that much more appealing. I wanted to be a part of their inner circle, to be included in their inside jokes, to share in their familiar camaraderie, if only for a few hours.

It might have been easier to take if they'd acted like the uneducated sex addicts they were supposed to be. But here in their natural environment, with the camera turned off and no expectations to live up to, they were surprisingly... well, *normal.* From what I could overhear, there were no explicit discussions of wild conquests or genital hygiene. Sex was never a topic of conversation. Instead, they discussed friends, family. Even the banality of their home lives was reminiscent of office co-workers gossiping at the water cooler, happy for a short break from their daily routines.

"I took my car to the shop today, and the guy tells me the transmission's screwed up. But I know that's bullshit cause I just had it checked."

"I warned you about buying used. I've got a buddy who

works at a Honda dealership. I'll hook you up."

"My parents are coming to town tomorrow."

"Oh no!"

"Yeah, I had all these plans for the weekend, and now I gotta spend it driving them around on one of those stupid star tours."

"You should take them down to Venice Beach. It's really nice this time of year."

There have been a lot of negative things said about porn, and not all of it is inaccurate. But the men and women I observed that day did not appear to be victims. Of course, a person doesn't end up in porn without having at least a few dark secrets in the past. Somewhere in their lives, they got mixed signals about sex. At some point, they deviated from the norm. But porn didn't create them.

Surprising as it may seem, hardly anybody in this industry didn't ask to be there. Stories of kidnappings or drugs used for coercion are, for the most part, just urban myths. The vast majority of actors actively sought out careers in porn, and fight like hell every day to remain there. One might argue that they just needed the money, and would gladly leave it all behind if they had any other option. But then again, one might also argue that McDonald's is always hiring.

In the end, money has very little to do with why so many wayward souls turn to porn. More than just a source of income, it's also a safe haven from an outside world that either has no use for them or openly despises them. Here they feel part of a larger community where they're accepted and surrounded by like-minded (and equally deviant) people. Argue all you want about objectification and degradation, there was nobody being beaten, raped or verbally abused on that set, the food was pretty damn good, and everybody left for the day with money in their pockets. Considering the alternatives, it was the best that a lot of them could hope for right now, including myself.

"Anybody sitting here?" I heard a voice ask.

I was so caught up in thought that it took a moment to realize this question was directed at me. I looked up and saw a completely naked woman standing there. She was a pretty brunette, skinny and athletic, with a tan like shellacked wood. But her most predominate feature was her enormous breasts, which seemed to inhabit their own area code.

"No, not at all," I said, with just a bit too much enthusiasm. "Go right ahead."

She sat down next to me and began picking at her food, nibbling on a piece of cauliflower like she intended to make it last for hours. "My name's Ginger," she said. "Aren't we working together today?"

I was going to tell her no, she must have mistaken me for somebody else. But at the last minute, I thought better of it. Each time I'd admitted to being a writer, I was greeted with cold stares and outright animosity. Just once I wanted to be perceived as something other than an outsider.

"I think so," I said.

"You're the new kid, right? Felipe?"

"Felipe, that's right," I said, wondering if it was too late to start using an accent.

"It's great to finally meet you. I've heard a lot of great things."

She winked at me, smiling with such reassuring tenderness that it almost made me want to weep openly.

"Are you still looking for an apartment?" she asked.

"Oh, yeah. No luck yet." So far this was easy enough, just so long as she kept asking questions that required a simple yes or no response.

"If you need a place to stay, you can crash on my couch," she offered.

I thanked her, and she returned to her meal. I tried to avert my eyes from her nudity but it was a losing battle. I wasn't accustomed to prolonged exposure to live female breasts, much less when they were so casually displayed. I began reading my script again, if only so I had something distracting to do with my hands.

"What do you think of the script?" I asked her.

She just shrugged. "It is what it is."

This was not the reaction I'd been hoping for. "It's pretty good though, don't you think? I mean, you don't usually find such high-quality scripts in our line of work."

"I didn't read it," she admitted. "I never do. They're all the same."

"I really think you should," I said, growing more insistent. "This one is different. The characters are complex and three dimensional, the plot has so many layers..."

She smirked. "You're kidding, right?"

I pushed my copy of the script across the table. She took it and began to read. She couldn't have finished more than half a page before she crinkled her nose in protest.

"Aw, hell," she said.

"What's wrong?"

"I told him I wasn't doing anal."

I was about to tell her that she was missing the point of that particular scene, but before I could open my mouth, Brandon wandered over and pushed his way into our booth. He was wearing only a towel and his chest was still wet from a post-sex shower.

"Well, looky here," he said. "The lion and the sheep have become friends. Will wonders never cease?"

"What are you talking about?" Ginger asked.

"I owe you a check," he said to me, and pulled out a checkbook from God knows where. "Who should I make it out to?"

I froze like a deer in headlights. Brandon and Ginger looked at me. I could feel my tongue getting dry, and I swallowed hard. Brandon wasn't just aware of the tension, he seemed to be enjoying it.

"Have you two formally met?" he finally inquired. "Ginger, this is Eric, one of our writers."

She recoiled in disgust. "A *writer*?" Her face developed a defiant hardness, and her eyes seemed to be burning through me. "Excuse me," she said curtly, and picked up her plate, retreating towards her friends at the other end of the room.

Brandon watched her go, then turned back to me. "Don't worry about her, sport. She's been in a bitchy mood all morning."

With that unpleasantness out of the way, Brandon returned to his checkbook. "Seriously, I want to pay you," he said. "You got a pen on you?"

I nodded, relieved that he didn't have a pen stashed somewhere in that towel. He wrote me a check for five hundred dollars, not bothering to ask my name again. When he handed me the check, it was a thrilling sensation. All this time, I hadn't really believed that I would actually be compensated. It was too easy, there had to be a catch. But there I was, holding legal proof that I had contributed some valuable service. It almost made it worth the psychological torture I'd had to endure.

"Are you going to stick around and watch some more?" Brandon said, returning his checkbook to parts unknown. "We're shooting the prison scene next."

This remark gave me pause. "What prison scene?" I asked.

"Oh, it's going to be hot," he went on. "Two girls and a guy. You haven't lived till you've seen Ginger in a skimpy prison guard outfit."

"I don't mean to meddle, but I don't think there's a prison scene in my script."

"No, there's not. But we already built the set and it'd be a shame to waste it."

"How are you going to make that work? I mean, it's completely out of context with the rest of the story."

"You think? I hadn't noticed."

"I'm sure you're a fine director, but—"

"Just wait till you see the set," he insisted. "It looks totally real. It's got bars on the windows and everything."

"That's not what I'm worried about."

"I know what you're worried about," he said, furrowing his brow. "And I wish I could help you. But we're on a tight budget here and I can't tear down a perfectly good prison set just because there doesn't happen to be a prison in the movie."

I could see his point. But the protective writer in me couldn't allow this to happen without trying to salvage what remained of my creative dignity.

"If you want," I said, "I could do a quick rewrite so that the scene makes more sense."

Brandon laughed, slapping the table to emphasize his enjoyment. "That is funny," he roared. "You see, that's why you're a great writer."

"I'm serious."

"And so am I. Finish your lunch and then come join us downstairs. You won't be disappointed."

He slid out of the booth but I didn't move. I just clutched my check, staring down at a script that was beginning to look more irrelevant to this process with each passing second.

The filming continued well into the afternoon and early evening, and I still didn't recognize anything that had originated from my script. I watched as black pimps in afros and frisky white cheerleaders were paraded before me, performing feats that could only be described as psychopathic proctology, and not once did I hear them utter even a single line of my carefully crafted dialogue. I was beginning to suspect that this had been the plan all along. Hiring a writer was just a formality, but in the end, all they really wanted was a string of unrelated sex scenes.

Eventually I asked Brandon if he had any intention of shooting my script. "We have to shoot the sex first," he said. "Once that's out of the way, we'll get to your stuff."

I tried to be patient, but I was becoming increasingly bored with the entire proceedings. I wandered in and out of the set, pointing angrily at my watch or clearing my throat at inopportune times. I came dangerously close to being banned from the premises when, after witnessing a lesbian tryst drag on for almost two hours, I pointed out to Brandon that the scene was rapidly becoming redundant.

As the clock approached midnight, Brandon finally called a wrap. But before the crew could pack up their cameras and run for the doors, Brandon reminded them that their day was not over. "Okay, people," he shouted. "Let's do the fast forward."

His announcement was greeted with groans of protest and gnashing of teeth. A gloomy fatigue fell over the room and the crew went about their tasks with exaggerated fatigue. One of the actresses walked onto the set, her hair in curlers, and asked me why everybody looked so upset.

"Something about a fast forward," I replied.

"Oh no, really?" the actress said, frowning deeply. "Shit, I hate this part."

"What's a fast forward?" I asked.

A grip walked over, dragging his feet like a teenager on his way to detention. "Fucking hell," he grumbled.

"I know," the actress agreed.

"It never gets any easier," the grip said.

Another actor joined the group. "Fast forward?" he said, noting their sour expressions.

"It's just not fair," the actress scowled.

"What's a fast forward?" I asked again.

"The script," the actor said, almost whispering the words.

"I don't get it," I said. "Why's it called 'fast forward'?"

They looked at me like I had missed something obvious. And then they each held up a hand, mimicking the use of a remote control. "Fucking fast forward," the grip moaned. "Like it matters."

The two leads walked onto the set, silently reviewing their scripts with worried faces. I recognized the man as Ian, the scruffy actor/ producer I'd met during my first meeting with Brandon. He was dressed in a lime green suit and silk shirt, unbuttoned to the waist. The woman, whom I would later learn went by the pseudonym "Sabrina," was tall and bony. She wore a sequin dress with velcro in the back for easy, one-step disrobing.

"Let's do this thing," Ian said, throwing his script to the ground.

Brandon yelled action, the cameras rolled, and for one brief, beautiful moment, my words breathed life. It was a short-lived victory. Only half a page into the script, Ian flubbed his line.

"Fuck," he growled, smacking the wall. "Let me try it again."

The second take wasn't much better, nor was the third or the fourth. He finally managed to say a line without garbling the words, which surprised him more than anybody, so much that he became disoriented and lost his place.

"What the shit?" Ian yelled. "I'm sorry, I don't know why I keep doing that."

"I think I see the problem," Brandon said. "You're relying too much on the exact words. If it helps, you can paraphrase it."

"Para-what?" Ian asked.

Brandon smiled, as if apologizing for his inconsiderate use of a big word. "Forget the script," he said. "Just say whatever comes to your head."

I bit my lip, or else I might have started screaming bloody murder. But as much as it pained me, I knew that this was probably the only reasonable option. I tried to tell myself that it would all work out for the best. Maybe Ian would at least be able to ad-lib some halfway decent dialogue.

But that was just wishful thinking. His attempt at improvisation was even more disastrous. It only seemed to confuse him, not being a creature of spontaneity. Ian voiced his frustration with a string of obscenities, and Brandon called for a short break.

"Stupid fucker," Ian mumbled as he reviewed his script. "Stop fucking around. You can do this. You the man. You the man."

As Ian continued with his abusive pep talk, Brandon huddled with Sabrina in the corner. She appeared to be upset about something, and I naturally assumed that it was Ian. But as they talked, they occasionally made furtive glances in my direction. Brandon nodded, squeezed her arm, and walked towards me.

"I've got some bad news," he said.

"What?" I asked.

"Sabrina is uncomfortable," he said. "She says can't perform with so many people staring at her."

"I see."

"She wants a closed set. Only the crew and production staff. I'm sorry, buddy. You know how actresses can be."

I had little choice but to accept her demands. This ship was going down fast, and I didn't want to be the cause of yet another crisis. I was turning to leave when Brandon picked up a box and thrust it at me.

"What's this?" I asked.

"The props," he said. "Congratulations. You're our new prop master."

The box was filled with wigs, bras, and a frightening assortment of sexual novelties. "I don't follow," I said.

"You want to stay and watch? You need a job. Just sit in the corner and wait for somebody to ask for a prop."

I did as I was told, though I felt slightly foolish. This was hardly what I'd bargained for. I was supposed to be the triumphant writer, relishing the fruits of his labor. Instead, I'd been bullied into the role of unpaid stagehand, crouched in the shadows with a box of dildos.

Ian was even more flustered when shooting began again. He started the scene promisingly enough but before he had a chance to speak, he appeared to lose all control of the muscles in his mouth. His entire body began to tremble and it looked like he might pass out from the strain. With his last ounce of strength, he managed to mutter a single word.

"Fuzzwubbit," he said.

The crew exploded with laughter. "What's a fuzzwubbit?" the cameraman giggled.

"Shut up," Ian grumbled, his face going suddenly red.

"I don't even think that's a word," one of the gaffers said.

"I said shut the fuck up," Ian shouted. "I made a mistake, okay?"

"Cut it out, guys," Brandon scolded the crew.

"Hey, writer dude," the cameraman said, turning to me. "Is 'fuzzwubbit' a real word?"

I felt a pang of sympathy for Ian. He was already embarrassed, he didn't need to be cruelly mocked for his verbal inadequacies. Had I been in a more generous mood, I might have done the noble thing and defended the poor simpleton. But I'd spent too much time being the outcast in this group and I was delighted that somebody else was finally on the receiving end of their hostility.

"I don't think so," I said. "It might be Pig Latin."

The laughter only got louder and Ian stormed out of the room, giving me a hateful glare as he left.

"Alright, I guess we're taking another break," Brandon said. "We'll let Ian cool down and try it again in five."

With some time to kill, I somehow found an exit door and sneaked outside for a quick smoke. But as the door slammed behind me, I realized that I'd inadvertently picked the exact stop where Ian had retreated for some privacy. I pulled at the door but it had locked behind me. Resigned to my fate, I reached for a cigarette and lit it, trying to seem preoccupied with my task. Though I was careful not to look directly at him, I could feel Ian's eyes on me, as if he was just waiting for an excuse to shove my face into the concrete.

"What are you looking at?" he snarled to my back.

"Nothing," I said, staring at my feet.

As I smoked my cigarette in silence, I decided that I was

tired of being afraid. I shouldn't have to cower in the shadows, careful not to make any sudden moves that might be misconstrued as aggressive. I was going to take a chance and initiate a conversation, even if it was likely to end in a violent confrontation.

"You want some help running lines?" I asked Ian, holding up my script as a sort of peace offering.

He paused, perhaps wondering if this was another thinly veiled joke at his expense. And then, satisfied that my intentions were friendly, he rewarded me with a begrudging smile.

"No," he said, "I got this shit down."

I tucked the script under my arms, making it clear that as far as I was concerned, the subject of his memorization skills was a dead topic. This put him at ease and he moved closer, though still keeping a safe distance between us.

"I keep thinking about it," he said, "and it pisses me off. It just ain't fair, y'know?"

I didn't have the slightest clue what he might be referring to, but I played along anyway. "It really isn't," I said.

He plucked the cigarette out of my hands and took a few short puffs. He smoked it like a joint, gulping in the smoke and holding it in until it seemed he might asphyxiate himself. He handed it back and I reluctantly accepted it, handling it like a piece of broken glass.

"What else do I gotta do to prove to them I'm ready?" he asked.

"They just don't get it," I muttered. "Bastards."

"I should walk out. Get in my car right now and leave. Then they'll see I mean business."

"I wouldn't do that." The last thing I needed was to lose my only male lead. That would be all the excuse Brandon needed to cut the script entirely. I wasn't about to let this boob ruin my movie without a fight.

He reached for my cigarette again, and I gladly let him have it. As he smoked the last of it, I reached into my pockets for the package of moist towelettes I'd brought for just such an occasion.

"You have a better idea?" he asked.

"Well," I said, thinking quickly. "Maybe I could talk to them."

Ian gazed at me with an expression of sincere gratitude. "You'd do that for me?"

"Oh, sure. I've been meaning to bring it up with them anyway."

It wasn't entirely untrue. If it meant saving the production, I would gladly talk to them. Now all I had to do was figure out who "they" were, and what Ian wanted them to know. A small technicality.

"I-I don't know what to say," Ian said, getting visibly choked up. "You really think I could be a good director?"

Now we were getting somewhere. "It's obvious you have an eye for it," I said, hoping he wouldn't make me back this up with examples.

"You think so?"

"You're like a young Tarantino."

"It was my idea to make *Pulp Friction*," he said, his voice rising. "They fucking stole it from me."

"If you ask me, it's about time you stopped letting these assholes take advantage of you. You're a major talent in this industry and you deserve to be treated as such."

"I'm the man!" he declared.

Ian pulled me close, hugging me with such ferocity that I feared he might break my spine. "Thanks, dude."

"Don't worry about it."

He released me and ran a forearm across his face. We stood there in silence, neither sure what to say or do next.

"You wanna go do some coke in the back of my van?" he finally said.

"Maybe later," I said. "But first you need to get back in there and finish what you started."

"You think I should?"

"I do. If you're going to be a director from now on, this could very well be your last performance. If I were you, I'd want to go out with a bang."

He hesitated, but soon the enormity of this occasion began to sink in. His face glowed with pride, and he lifted a fist into the air, giving me a victorious salute.

"Rock and roll!" he screamed, and ran towards the door. He opened it easily, though I could have sworn it was locked. He paused, holding the door open, but I motioned for him to go on without me.

"Aren't you coming?" he asked.

"I'll be there in a minute," I said.

When he was gone, I turned and walked towards the parking lot. I would have liked to stay a little longer but it was getting late and I wanted to get home before my wife started to worry.

As I opened the door to my car, I remembered that I'd left the box of props unattended inside. No matter, I thought. They can get another dildo-boy.

My work here was done.

5

My wife had stopped talking to me.

It started when I returned from the video shoot, and had gotten progressively worse ever since. I thought she was just upset that I had spent an entire day leering at naked women. Certainly she knew me well enough to know that I'd never dream of cheating on her, especially not with some surgically-altered porn actress who was likely infected with any number of STDs.

To be honest, it was no mystery why she was really upset. In an unlucky coincidence, the date of the video shoot just so happened to fall on her birthday. We had made plans to celebrate that night, and I'd promised to return in plenty of time to take her out on the town. But due to circumstances beyond my control, I didn't stumble home until early that next morning, only to find that she had already gone to bed. I'd brought her a present, a prop that I'd stolen from the set, but this didn't seem to make her any happier. The next morning I tried to explain why I'd been delayed but she would have none of it. In what was to be her final communication, she informed me that if porn was so important to me, I would have to live without her affections.

I endured her silent treatment for almost a week, and still she showed no sign of forgiveness. Surely I had been punished enough — her point had been made — and it was time to end this madness. I waited until we were driving to the supermarket on our weekly grocery exposition. This way, I reasoned, she wouldn't be able to ignore me so easily. She was trapped, and unless she wanted to fling herself onto the highway, she'd be forced to hear me out.

"You still love me?" I asked, lightly touching her shoulder.

She roughly pushed me away, nearly swerving off the road. "Don't talk to me," she snapped.

"I'm sorry. How many times do I have to say I'm sorry?"

She flipped on the radio, turning it up to an ear-piercing volume. I could beg all I wanted, she wasn't going to grant me absolution today. I sighed and eased back into my seat. Okay then, I thought, two can play at this game. Brandon's check was still in my pocket and I had planned to deposit it today. But if she wanted to continue punishing me, then she could live without the money. I didn't care if it meant our utilities would be shut off, it would be worth it if I could convince her that I was not the bad guy.

We wandered through the supermarket, silently collecting groceries and exchanging icy glares. And then, just when it seemed that things couldn't get any more miserable, we turned a corner and came face to face with our past.

"Spitzy? Is that really you?"

It was Scott, a mutual friend from Chicago. The last we'd heard, he was still a regular performer at the Second City, a comedy club where my wife and I had been briefly employed as writing teachers. He was one of our first students and we'd encouraged him to audition for the mainstage company, for which he'd been immediately hired.

Working at a comedy institution like the Second City could be both a blessing and a curse. On the one hand, its roster of famous alumni reads like a *Who's Who* of comedy. Mike Myers, Bill Murray and Gilda Radner had all begun their careers there. It was quite inspiring to be surrounded by so much raw potential. On any given day, you could be reasonably sure that at least half the people you met were almost destined to become rich and successful.

But potential is always better than reality. The last thing that anybody wants is to bump into an old student who has somehow managed to become more rich and successful than you.

"I didn't know you were in L.A.," Scott said. "How long have you been here?"

We exchanged mild pleasantries and he informed us that he had recently joined the cast of an immensely popular TV sketch show. We smiled and congratulated him though inside we were both secretly wishing that he would come down with a terminal case of bowel cancer. Not that he wasn't talented, but he was also at least five years younger than the both of us. Couldn't he have at least waited for us to achieve some degree of success first? It was only fair.

"So what's been happening for you?" he asked.

We were in no mood to share the details of our uneventful lives, especially after hearing of his good fortune. "Oh, not much," I said. "I'm still tinkering with a novel. And my agent is shopping around a screenplay."

"That's great," he said, with forced enthusiasm.

"You're not going to tell him?" my wife asked with a wry grin.

We both turned to her. "Tell me what?" Scott asked.

"He's writing porn," she said, nudging me.

"Holy Christ!" was Scott's reaction.

I couldn't believe it. My own wife had exposed me. I knew she was still angry but this was borderline marital abuse. "It's nothing, really," I said, nearly choking on the words. "It's just a little something I'm doing on the side to pay the bills."

Scott's eyes were almost bursting from their sockets. "You have to tell me everything," he said.

"There's nothing to tell." I shot my wife a desperate look.

"How'd you get the gig?" Scott asked. "What's your script about? Have you seen any naked boobies yet? Don't leave anything out."

As if on cue, Scott's wife appeared from around the corner. Her name was Tina and, like her husband, she was an actress on a completely unfair winning streak. Not only was she a cast member on the aforementioned sketch show, but she also had a supporting role on a highly rated sitcom on the WB. My wife greeted her with a hug, though her eyes told me that she wanted nothing more than to watch this woman ripped apart by wild dogs.

"Spitz is writing porn," Scott announced, loud enough for most of the store to hear.

"For real?" she said, slapping me on the shoulder.

Once again, I was grilled for all the usual details. But Tina and Scott didn't stop there. They asked questions that were so specific, they betrayed an intimate knowledge with the inner workings of the porno industry.

"Are you doing gonzos or features?" Tina said.

"Of course he's doing features," Scott sniffed. "That's where the real money is."

"Who's your director? Please tell me it's Tom Byron. I love his work."

"I think he's under contract with Excalibur Films."

"I read somewhere that Wicked and Excalibur were going to merge."

"The trades have been saying that for months. It isn't going to happen."

"It'd be a good move for Wicked. Ever since they lost Jenna Jameson, their stock has been dropping."

I've always wondered why comedians know so much about porn. I've been known to socialize with more than a few of them in my time, and I have yet to meet one who didn't have an encyclopedic knowledge of the smut trade. In fact, in some comedy circles, the mere mention of the names Peter North or the Dark Brothers will spark a round-table discussion that could last for hours. It may be because most comics are products of rejection and isolation. But I suspect that they are just naturally attracted to any art form that, by definition, is so open to ridicule that it just never bothered to put up a fight.

When the questioning ended, Tina and my wife continued down the aisle with their carts, chatting affably about the latest Hollywood gossip. I saw my chance and pulled Scott aside. I wanted to ask him about his TV show, specifically its writing staff.

"Would you put in a good word for me?" I said. "Maybe mention my name to the head writer?"

"Forget that," he said, dismissing me with a wave. "What do

you want with our little show? You're in the big leagues now."

He winked at me and chuckled. I joined in his laughter but quickly cut it short. "Seriously," I said. "I could use your help. The porn thing is okay, but it's not like I want to make a career of it."

"Don't tell me you're thinking of giving it up?" he said, utterly confounded. "Are you nuts? Do you know how many people in this town secretly wish they were doing porn instead?"

"I doubt that," I said.

"Trust me. Don't take it for granted. I mean, I love doing the TV thing. But it's fleeting. It doesn't last. What you've got, it's *real*."

"How so?"

"Twenty years from now, I'll just be a footnote in pop culture. But you have the chance for real permanence. You could be the next Gerard Damiano, the next Artie Mitchell, the next *Seymore Butts.*"

He spoke the names with a hushed reverence, but they meant nothing to me.

"Besides," he continued, "you want to write comedy, right? Some of the greatest comedy films ever made were pornos. What was that one Jerry Stahl did in the early '80s? Not *Café Flesh*, the other one."

"You mean *Night Dreams*?" I asked. "Was that really a comedy?"

"Are you kidding me? Have you even *seen* it? The scene where Dorothy LeMay has sex with a huge Cream of Wheat box is pure comedy gold. It's a stroke of cinematic genius."

I just shrugged. "If you're into that sorta thing."

"Think about it," he said. "You're a lucky guy. I'd trade places with you in a heartbeat."

"It's a deal."

"Don't tempt me."

We both laughed at our little joke, though I'm fairly sure that neither one of us was entirely kidding.

"I've been in this business twenty fucking years," Ray snarled. "And I've never had somebody try to fuck me like this before."

Ray paced his office, swinging at the air with a golf club. For the moment at least, his rage was not directed at me, for which I was immensely grateful. When Ray called earlier that morning, suggesting that it was time for us to meet face to face, I was convinced that he had just grown tired of yelling at me over the phone and wanted to do it in person.

I arrived for our meeting well ahead of schedule, only to discover that the address he'd given me belonged to a meatpacking plant. After speaking with various gruff men in blood-stained overalls, I learned that Ray's office was in the back. I assumed that he was just leasing the space and his porn company wasn't being subsidized by the beef industry. I wandered through a maze of raw meat, hopelessly lost. I have a terrible sense of direction as it is, but navigating through rows of nearly identical cow carcasses was an exercise in futility. For all I knew, I'd been walking in circles for hours.

I finally located the right door, and walked into a tiny office that was decorated like a frat house bachelor pad circa 1983. The walls were lined with framed Patrick Nagel posters, a leopard-skin couch barely concealed a fold-out bed, and thick shag carpeting covered most of the floor. The lighting was minimal at best, and the gentle rhythms of New Age music played softly over a stereo system.

I was sitting on the edge of the couch, poised for a hasty

retreat should it become necessary. Ray continued to swing his club, as if practicing for a brutal beating. Despite his violent outbursts, he wasn't nearly as intimidating as I'd been expecting. He appeared to be in his early to mid 40s, although he dressed like a man half his age. His hair was short and bleached to a perfect white, and a trimmed goatee was barely visible against his pale complexion. He was wearing a neon orange Hawaiian shirt and combat boots, and a phone headset was strapped to his head. The whole look suggested retired teen pop crooner more than porn auteur with vicious temper.

"I refuse to take this shit lying down," Ray howled. "Get her on the fucking phone, I'll fucking talk to her."

Clark, the company's producer, was standing nearby, watching his partner with a concerned expression. He was older than Ray and showed his age. His skin had a leathery texture like a weathered piece of furniture from a second-hand store. His mostly dark hair was graying at the temples, and his mustache was badly in need of a trim. An old band-aid, which had long since lost any adhesive properties, was loosely affixed to his neck, hanging on for dear life. He at least dressed like an adult, though his suit appeared to be at least as ancient as he was.

"It's not that simple," Clark said in a calm voice. "You can't bully her on this. Our hands are tied."

"Fucking bitch doesn't know who she's fucking dealing with."

The "bitch" in question was the Stockholm actress with the prosthetic leg, who until a few hours ago was to be the star of our film. But we'd just received a press release from her manager, announcing that she was retiring from the business immediately. No explanation was given, other than that she would be "pursuing other interests." Personally, I didn't see why this was cause for concern. With such an overabundance of women in southern California clamoring for screen time, some of them with all of their original limbs, surely we could find a replacement. But Ray was clearly not a man accustomed to being told "No."

Ray took a final swing with his club and threw it to the ground. His teeth clenched as he struggled to contain his rage. "Fuuuuck!" he screamed.

Clark cringed, as he did every time Ray swore. He seemed honestly uncomfortable with Ray's frequent use of expletives. "This is easily fixable," he said. "We'll just use one of the contract girls."

The "contract girl" was still a new concept to me. As I understood it, the majority of porn actresses are hired strictly on a freelance basis. At best, they can expect to make as much as $150 per scene. At worst, they're lucky to get cab fare. But in that rare occurrence when an actress becomes a recognizable name, a video company will invite her to sign an exclusive contract in which she agrees to headline a certain number of films in exchange for a larger salary and all the perks (e.g., a dressing room) that come with quasi-celebrity.

"I don't want to use a goddamn contract girl," Ray snarled. "The public wants a fresh face. Fucking bitch, fucking thinks she can fucking screw me. Fuck the fucking fucker!"

"Would you please stop with the potty mouth, please?"

I hadn't known him long but already I could tell that Clark was in the wrong line of work. His aversion to cursing was one thing, but when a grown man uses a phrase like "potty mouth," it's a fairly good indicator that he isn't cut out for a career in porn. Adorable though it was, his attitude seemed a bit prudish for somebody who made his living in exposed genitals. I would have given anything to watch him lose his temper and unleash a tirade of tame cussing. "Shoot! This is a load of poop! Gosh darn it, f-ing heck!"

"Let's talk about something else," Clark said. "You've got the writer here, let's discuss the script."

Ray seemed to suddenly realize that I was in the room. This pleased him considerably, if only because he now had a physical target on which to unleash his wrath. He picked up a copy of the script from his desk and hurled it, aiming for my head.

"It's shit," he snapped.

I ducked just in time. The script hit the wall and fluttered miserably to the floor. Clark ran over to retrieve it.

"It's not shit," he said, giving Ray a disapproving glare. "It just needs a little editing."

Clark sat next to me on the couch and gently smoothed out the script's crumpled pages. Even before Ray had used it as a projectile weapon, it had apparently endured considerable abuse at his hands.

"We had to cut a few lines." He flipped through the script, pointing out dialogue that had been crossed out in thick red ink. "Here... and here... and here."

By the time Clark finished, I wondered if there was anything in my draft that he intended to keep. He had cut quite a bit more than "a few lines." Entire scenes were gone, scenes that I once believed to be integral to the plot. Most of the characters had been eliminated and those that remained had precious little to say. I didn't actually count but if I were to wager a guess, I'd say that my entire script had been slashed to approximately one paragraph.

"I assume you'll be wanting another rewrite," I said.

"If you wouldn't mind," Clark replied.

"It'd help if I could get a better idea of what you need."

"Oh, that's simple. We need twenty pages."

I waited for him to elaborate but he just stared back at me, satisfied that he'd provided me with all the information I could possibly require.

"Do you not like the characters?" I asked.

"No, of course not. The characters are great."

"Does the plot make sense?"

"Perfectly. We love it."

"So you want..."

"Twenty pages, yes."

My head was beginning to throb. "Of what?" I asked.

"Just twenty pages."

I should have stopped right there. Clearly, we were speaking a different language. But I hoped that if I could just keep him talking, eventually he would slip up and tell me something useful.

"You want me to change the dialogue?"

"Have you not been fucking listening?" Ray interjected. "Didn't Clark just take an ax to your fucking precious fucking dialogue?"

"Raymond, please." Clark folded his hands, carefully considering his words before proceeding. "For our purposes, dialogue tends to get in the way."

"So in these twenty pages," I said, "what's going to be happening?"

"Pretty much the same. We think you really nailed it."

"But no one's talking?" I asked.

"Talking about what?" Clark replied.

Ray smiled at Clark with smug conviction, as if I had just proven my incompetence beyond any doubt. "I told you this fucker was a troublemaker," he said.

Was it me? Had I misunderstood a perfectly reasonable request? I didn't think so. This wasn't merely a matter of creative differences. It wasn't conflicting views on what constitutes good storytelling. What he was asking from me was impractical. A mathematical impossibility. But as obvious as this seemed, they couldn't see it. Their brains refused to accept it. And I didn't even know where to begin making them understand. It would have been like explaining quantum physics to a classroom of pre-school children.

"I'm just not sure what it is you want me to do," I said. "I can't write a twenty page script without dialogue. Unless you want twenty blank pages."

Clark was looking deeply troubled. He must have realized just how flawed his logic was and could no longer find the words to defend it. His world — his entire creative philosophy — was crumbling in front of him and the vacant look in his eyes showed just how desperately he wanted it back. Ray must have sensed it too because he grabbed for his golf club and advanced towards me menacingly.

"You know what your fucking problem is?" he said, stopping just short of the couch. "You can't think outside the box."

"How so?" I knew it was foolhardy to challenge the intellect of a man brandishing a golf club but I wasn't about to back down so easily.

He paced the room, swinging his club into the air as he thought. Suddenly, he turned and pointed a finger at me excitedly. "You ever see that film *In Like Flint*?"

"Yeah," I said. "With James Coburn, right?"

"Make it like that. Chicks running around in their skivvies, doing judo, jumping on trampolines, all that crazy shit."

It wasn't much to go on but it was a start. "Okay, I can do that," I said, furiously writing on the back of my script. "But it still doesn't help me with—"

"If you run into any more problems," he continued, "just use that outline I gave you."

I glanced at my notes from our last phone conversation. "A master bedroom, a lighthouse, a tennis court, two pools, and a gazebo," I repeated.

"There you go."

This seemed to satisfy Clark and his confidence quickly returned. "You're doing fine," he said, slapping me on the back. "We have complete faith in you."

Although I wasn't any closer to figuring out what they expected, I wasn't about to challenge Clark again. It was a losing battle. I could grill them all day and I still wouldn't get anything coherent out of them.

"You fucking gimp bitch! I'll fucking kill you!"

At first, I thought Ray was screaming at me. But then Clark lunged at him and reached for the microphone on his phone headset. "Ray, I told you not to call her!"

Ray slapped his hand away and scurried across the room. "We had a verbal agreement, goddammit!" he roared, as Clark continued to chase him. "I'll have you fucking deported! I'll beat you to fucking death with your own fucking leg!"

Ray wasn't exactly spry on his feet but he knew how to play dirty. He would occasionally knock over a chair or throw a lamp in Clark's path, which was all the advantage he needed. When they had nearly trashed the office, Clark finally caught up with him. He grabbed Ray at the knees and they tumbled to the ground.

After restraining Ray with a powerful chokehold, Clark managed to pull away the headset. "Don't listen to him!" he yelled into the microphone. "He has no authority!"

"The fuck I don't!" Ray roared.

Ray kneed his partner in the groin and they rolled across the floor, slapping and biting each other. The pungent odor of sweat and cologne was thick. Combined with the stench of raw beef coming from just outside their door, I was beginning to feel slightly nauseous.

Ray broke free just long enough to grab his golf club, and took a swing at Clark's head, missing him by inches. His next swing missed Clark entirely but came so close to my face that a sharp breeze sent me flying backwards.

"Rue the day!" he bellowed. "Rue the fucking day, you fucking cocksucker!"

Clark and Ray escorted me to the parking lot, having decided to go out for a late lunch. I was not invited, for which I was greatly relieved. No further mention was made of their violent scuffle. It was as if the whole thing had never happened or, even more disturbing, was just a normal part of their business day.

"You want to try that new sushi place?" Clark asked.

"I hate fucking sushi," Ray said, scratching his rug-burned cheek. "I want to eat something that doesn't fucking remind me of work."

I spotted my car and tried to slip away unnoticed. But as I fumbled for my keys, I could feel Clark's skeletal fingers on my back.

"You need any help at all," he whispered, "give me a call, okay?"

He continued to gaze at me as if he wanted to say more. And then his eyes drifted to my car. His face dropped so suddenly, I thought he must have seen something horrible. Maybe there was blood on my windshield or the body of a child affixed to the front bumper. I turned, but it was just as I'd left it. I drove an old Honda that, admittedly, wasn't easy on the eyes. It had a few nicks and rust patches, and the front taillight had long since caved in. But it worked well enough for my purposes.

I noticed that Ray was also staring at my car with the same baffled look on his face. He and Clark exchanged a glance and then turned back to me. Their expressions were unmistakable. It was pity. They were embarrassed for me. I could hardly believe it. *They* were embarrassed for *me*. These men who made their living in porn somehow felt they had the right to judge me. And for my *car*, no less. I might have expected as much from a well-established agent or producer who at least had the Hollywood status to justify their feelings of superiority. But this was unacceptable. So what if my car was a piece of shit? I was still higher on the evolutionary food chain than they could ever hope to be.

"Nice wheels," Ray snickered. My moral indignation didn't stand a chance against their merciless sneering. I gave them an abrupt wave and climbed inside my Honda. As I waited for them to leave, I found my cellphone and pretended to make a call. I just wanted to prove that I possessed at least one toy of the Hollywood elite. I chatted animatedly with my imaginary caller, certain that Ray and Clark were still watching. And then, as if the universe itself was trying to punish me, the cellphone rang.

I was mortified. I'd been exposed as a fraud and there was no way I'd ever get the upper hand again. I punched madly at the cellphone keys, trying to stop that infernal ringing. After several excruciating seconds, I finally hit the right one and muttered a timid greeting.

The voice on the other end belonged to Tim, my writer friend and the very person who'd gotten me into this mess in the first place. I hadn't heard from him since our ill-fated conversation in which he'd convinced me that writing porn would be a wise career move. I wanted to tear into him but something made me hold back. He sounded tense, almost scared.

"I think my video came out," he said.

I could only assume that he was referring to porn. If Tim had managed to sell a screenplay that didn't include hardcore sex, I doubt if he would have waited so long to tell me.

"Really? Congratulations."

I could hear Tim's labored breathing. "You haven't seen it, have you?"

"I don't think so. What's it called?"

"Beats me. They've changed the title so many times, it could be anything at this point."

He tried to describe the plot but couldn't be sure what of his original script had made it into the final cut. "I think there's a prison scene," he said. "I didn't actually *write* a prison scene but... well, it's a long story."

He hardly needed to explain. It was all eerily familiar and I wondered if I would be in his shoes soon enough. I knew that the life of a screenwriter could be difficult. I'd heard plenty of horror stories about the lack of respect given to writers in this town. It was no secret that a scribe could expect to have his creative input ignored and his scripts revised without consent. Some of them would even consider themselves lucky to get a ticket to their own advance screenings. But this seemed a bit excessive. At the very least, a writer should be able to find out when his film is being released and what the title might be. It didn't seem like much to ask for.

"You should call Brandon," I said. "He'd probably be able to get you a copy."

"Oh no, I'm not talking to that nut-job again."

It was a peculiar thing to say, especially considering that this was a man whom Tim had once emphatically advised me to contact. "What happened?" I asked, though I knew I didn't really want to find out.

"He asked me to write another script for him," Tim said. "Some porno remake of *The Seven Samurai*. Can you believe it?"

I could indeed believe it but I thought better of giving him any specifics. Instead, I told him about my run-in with Scott, the "TV star" who had professed his jealousy over our porn ventures. I hoped he'd find this encouraging news or, at the very least, some reason to feel that we weren't both the butt of some cosmic joke.

"Well, of course he'd say that," Tim sniffed. "It always looks better from a safe distance, doesn't it? If he could see it from our perspective, he'd realize just what an ugly, soul-sucking business it really is."

"When did you get so bitter?"

"It's *porn*, Spitz. Never forget that. There's nothing respectable about it."

"Have you forgotten that you talked me into doing this? You said—"

"I said write *one* script. One is fine. It makes a great anecdote. But I don't think either of us are stupid enough to make this a full-time job."

"Yeah, but—"

"It's like homosexuality. Try it once, you're just dabbling. But twice, and it's a lifestyle choice."

"I suppose."

"Just forget about it. We did it, we're done, let's move on.

Just be thankful that we got out before it was too late."

"Too late for what?"

"Too late to escape. You want to be a real writer, don't you? You can't do that if you get a reputation for making dirty movies. This town doesn't forgive indiscretions that easily."

"Yeah, but—"

"You've got to consider what future generations will think," Tim implored. "Everything we do affects our creative legacy. When it comes time for a retrospective of your career, how do you want them to remember you? Too much time in porn can mean the difference between having your life documented in an A&E *Biography* and an E! *True Hollywood Story*."

"B-but Jerry Stahl..."

"What about him? He was one of the lucky ones. And he could always blame it on the drugs. But for the rest of us, you stay in porn too long, you're trapped there forever."

I'd never had a panic attack before so I wasn't entirely sure what the symptoms were. This certainly felt like it. My palms were sweating, my heart was pounding against my ribcage, and my entire lower half had gone numb. Worse still, I had an overwhelming sensation of existential dread. I tried to focus my eyes but everything was a dizzy blur. I placed a hand on the steering wheel, bracing myself in case I should pass out.

"Are you still there?" Tim asked. "What's wrong?"

I couldn't speak. My tongue felt like hot lead, and swallowing was painful at best. I should have just hung up the phone but I didn't want Tim to know that he'd hit a nerve.

"Fuzzwubbit," I mumbled.

6

"You know what really makes me laugh? When people say that pornography objectifies women. That is such a crock. If anybody is being objectified, it's the *man*. Look at the average porno and you'll always see the woman's face. But the guy is only shown from the waist down. He's just a cock and balls, an anonymous torso with moving parts. Now you tell me, who's the one being portrayed as an object?"

The man sitting across from me had been talking nonstop for what seemed like hours and I was beginning to wonder why I'd agreed to meet him in the first place. When he called me — introducing himself only as "Stanley X" — he claimed to be a journalist for a popular adult video magazine. He'd seen my movie, he said, which surprised me because it had been less than a week since it went into production. He asked to take me out to lunch for an interview and I didn't hesitate to say yes. After what my ego had endured lately, I was looking forward to a free meal and the chance to share my insights on the writing craft to a willing listener.

Thus far, he'd done all of the talking and I hadn't even seen a menu yet.

"Another thing," Stanley continued, "I still don't understand what the big deal is about objectification anyway. I objectify half the people I meet in an average day. I go to McDonald's, I objectify the register guy. He's not a human being with emotions. He's the *object* that gets me food. I go to a rock concert and the singer is an *object* that entertains me. I don't care what he's feeling or whether he's in the mood to perform at that particular moment. I want to be entertained and then I want him to go away. And what's so wrong with that?"

"Well, I—"

"There are too many people in this world. We just don't have the time to get to know them all. We don't have a choice but to perceive most of them as objects. I'm not saying we should treat them like objects. Human beings aren't our personal playthings. But as far as I'm concerned, they're background players. I don't need to know their life story. I see them, I interact with them, and then they're gone. And that's the way it should be."

Stanley reminded me more of an accountant than a man who made his living watching and reviewing adult movies. His face was red and pinched, and he squinted as if he was staring directly into the sun. His body was covered in soft, hairless baby fat, and he looked awkward in his clothes, like a pet that'd been dressed in formalwear by an over-affectionate owner.

"The real problem isn't objectification at all," he said. "It's *sexual* objectification. We're afraid of sex and we always have been. You can argue all you want about how our country was founded on the freedom of personal expression. But in the end, we've never been comfortable with too much freedom when it comes to sex. I mean, we like to think we invented pornography but the ancient Romans were doing it long before we came along. If we brought anything new to erotica, it's censorship and sexual neurosis. We have Ed Meese to thank for that. As a nation, we have a clinical case of eurotophobia."

"What's that?" I asked.

"The fear of female genitalia. Look at our media, our politics, our *religions*, for Christ's sake. We're absolutely terrified of the pussy. We'd have every woman's vagina sewed closed at birth, if we could. And that's why we really hate pornography, isn't it? Too many cunts."

He signaled to the waiter and ordered appetizers for both of us, mostly vegan dishes that involved some variation on hummus. As he chatted with the waiter with whom he seemed to be on friendly terms, I glanced around the restaurant. By L.A. standards, it was a dive. But its location in downtown Canoga Park made it the preferred eatery for every porn professional living within a ten-mile radius.

I recognized a startling number of faces in the mid-day crowd. Ron Jeremy was sitting at a corner booth, surrounded by his entourage and other hangers-on. Tera Patrick was sharing hushed words with a lawyer at a table near the kitchen. Brittany Andrews and an older man who looked like John Leslie were gathering their coats and laughing at some private joke.

I knew I shouldn't be staring at them, but a part of me — the dark, dirty part — was starstruck. I was in the midst of porn greatness, watching them graze in their natural habitat. This was where they came to relax and socialize, to make deals or negotiate contracts. But most of all, it was *the* place to be seen. It was like one of those studio commissaries from the '40s, where you might find Jimmy Stewart eating alongside Groucho Marx and Katherine Hepburn.

"I know what you're thinking," Stanley said, raising his voice. "If it's so hopeless, why debate the issue? Well, my friend, I'm here to tell you that times are changing. Perceptions of pornography are evolving. It's a slow process but it is happening. Ed Meese is yesterday's news and the public is starting to realize that the taboo of adult cinema is antiquated and silly."

I peered at his tape recorder. He was still recording our conversation though I wasn't sure why. He hadn't asked me anything yet and hadn't even allowed me to get a word in edgewise. I took a sip from my glass of ice water and scanned the room for more psuedo-celebrities.

"Porn isn't the back alley business it was twenty years ago. It's moving into the mainstream. It's only a matter of time before budgets start ballooning and adult films become more artistically and commercially viable. We're already a competitive force in the marketplace and I guarantee you that in our lifetime porn will move out of the video stores and back into the theaters, where they belong."

"Isn't that what got Paul Reubens into trouble?" I asked with a sly grin. I was trying to be funny but Stanley either didn't get it or didn't find me all that humorous.

"Did you know that *Caligula* was made for seventeen million dollars?" he demanded, ignoring my remark. "And that was back in 1980. Thank God for Bob Guccione. We need more filmmakers like him. The critics can bitch and moan all they want but the public loves an event film. All we need is one more movie like that, one film with a bloated budget and marquee stars, and you'll see a weekend gross that makes *Titanic* look like an indie flick."

Our food arrived, and none too soon. My stomach was beginning to grumble and I needed some distraction from this babbling fool. I reached for a plate covered in brown goo and began shoveling it into my mouth.

"I know it sounds like I'm being naïve," Stanley continued, ignoring the food. "But you know what? Porn invented the box office smash. *Deep Throat* made one hundred *million* dollars in its initial theatrical release. And it cost only twenty-two grand to make. That makes it the highest budget-to-box-office ratio of any film ever. Forget *Jaws*. Forget *Jurassic Park*. Forget the whole goddamn *Star Wars* trilogy. When it comes to through-the-roof movie grosses, porn set the standard by which all others are judged."

I could hear excited murmuring coming from the other tables. All eyes were on the restaurant's entrance and a few people were even pointing. I turned around, fully expecting to see yet another porn megastar. But the man standing there was not anybody I recognized from adult films. He looked familiar but I couldn't place where I'd seen him before. He vaguely resembled one of those kids from *Saved By the Bell* except all grown up and graying at the temples. He may have been a Corey but I couldn't be certain. All I knew was that he definitely wasn't a regular here. From the way he was greeted with disbelieving awe, he might as well have been visiting royalty.

He swaggered over to an open table, well aware that he was the center of attention and enjoying every minute of it. But the crowd soon lost interest. And then, just as quickly, they began to sneer. It didn't take them long to become suspicious of why this foreigner would venture so far from his home turf. He was a Hollywood has-been, who had long ago lost his clout in L.A. proper. Rather than accepting obscurity, he had come to the

Valley, where he could more easily steal the spotlight. He was intruding on their world, taking away some of their celebrity. And they resented him for it.

"And that's why we're going to put you on our cover."

My head jolted back towards Stanley. He hadn't taken any notice of the mystery guest and must have kept right on talking. I had managed to tune him out but now I wished that I'd paid closer attention.

"You're what?" I asked.

"I know. It's exciting, isn't it? The publisher tried to fight me on this. He doesn't think our readership cares about some unknown porn writer. All he knows is tits and ass. But we'll show him, right?"

I shifted nervously in my seat. "Maybe that's not such a good idea."

"I've already got the perfect banner headline." He framed the air with his hands. " 'Eric Spitznagel: The New Face of Porn!' " He looked at me for a reaction, smiling broadly. "We're going to make you a star. You'll be our industry's poster child, the voice of the next generation. From now on, when people think of porn, I want them to think of you."

"I don't know if—"

"You think I do this for everybody? I watch hundreds of videos every week and most of them are terrible. But when I saw the rough cut of your film, I was blown away. Literally speechless. You understand the difference between erotica and just plain old smut. It's like what Carl Jung said: 'The brain is an appendage of the genitals.' Or was it Freud? I forget, but you see what I mean."

The terror was paralyzing. After my phone conversation with Tim, it'd taken a lot of soul-searching to convince myself that I wasn't yet doomed. I had wandered too deep into the porn tar pits, I knew that now. But it wasn't too late to crawl back to safety. There was nothing to prove my involvement. It was their word against mine and I would deny everything until my dying day.

But I hadn't counted on this. I hadn't expected the porn media to expose me. I honestly thought that as long as you remained behind the camera, your anonymity would be respected. Never in a million years did I anticipate that they would come clamoring for my photograph, threatening to publish the tawdry details of my literary misdeeds. If that happened, it would be all over. They'd have tangible evidence of my crimes.

Tim was right. The lucky ones got out while they had the chance. I'd been a fool.

"If it's all the same," I said. "I'd rather not do this."

Stanley fixed me with a blank stare. "I don't understand."

"I don't want you to write this article. If you wouldn't mind, let's just forget the whole thing."

"Now, hold on a minute. We're not just talking about some blurb in the back of the magazine. I'm offering you the *cover*."

"I know. I appreciate it, I really do. But I'm not interested."

"Have you talked to your publicist about this?"

"I don't have a publicist."

"Well, there's your problem, right there. I know some people, I can make a few calls."

"No, that's okay. I don't need a publicist. I just want to be left alone."

"Forgive me for saying so, but that's an ignorant way to build a career. You've got so much potential. If you play your cards right, you could become a household name. You could be the next Jerry Stahl, but without the mainstream cop-out. I'm talking awards, production deals, your own office."

"I think I can live without it."

Stanley stroked his chin, giving my request careful thought. "No," he finally said. "I'm sorry. I can't do this. I won't let you sabotage your career. I'm writing the story."

"Please don't."

"It's for your own good. In time, you'll thank me."

"I'll pay you." I was as surprised as he was to hear myself say those words.

"You'll what?" he asked.

I reached into my pocket and pulled out the check that Brandon had given me. I'm not sure why I hadn't cashed it yet. I'd long since proven to my wife that "dirty porn money" was as good as any other, and we were starting to get angry calls from collection agencies. There was no good reason not to pay off at least few of our debts. But for some reason, I held onto the check. It was as if I'd been waiting for just such an emergency.

"Five hundred dollars," I said, waving the check at him. "I'll sign it over to you right now if you promise never to put my name in print."

Stanley looked at me with disbelief. "You're nuts."

"Maybe. But what do you care? You're getting paid for doing nothing."

"I'd be lying if I didn't say I was insulted," he huffed. "This is bribery. If I accepted your money, I'd be violating every sacred code of journalistic ethics. It may not mean much to you but I couldn't live with myself if I betrayed that oath. I'm sorry, sir, but my integrity is not for sale."

"I was a journalist once. I know what it's like. And I know how difficult it can be to make a decent living on a magazine salary. Consider this a gift from one writer to another."

There was a short and uncomfortable silence as Stanley considered what to do. I could tell I was breaking him. He was looking for an excuse to snatch that check away from me. I just had to push him harder, find his weakness.

"Take some time off," I said. "Work on that novel. Or write a screenplay."

His eyes lit up. "I do have a script idea that I've been kicking around," he said.

"Well, here's your chance to finish it. Isn't it about time you stopped writing *about* porn and started writing *for* it?"

I placed the check on the table and slid it towards him. He looked at it, licking his lips. His head stayed down but the eyes swung towards me. He was giving me one final chance to take it back. When I did nothing, I could see him flexing his hands like a gunslinger at a Mexican standoff.

"Okay," he said. "You've got a deal."

In one swift movement, he seized the check and it disappeared into his jacket. We both leaned back in our chairs, exhausted but relieved. He smiled at me, shaking his head like he had just pulled off a brilliant con and had gotten away scot-free.

"I still think you're a crazy bastard," he said. "But I like you."

My brother was the first to tell me. "Hey," he said. "I just saw your porno."

"What are you talking about?"

He'd called from New York, where he did something in finance though I'm not sure what. "I was flipping through the TV," he said, "and they were showing it on the Spice channel."

"That's impossible."

He described the plot and it sounded like my script, added prison scene and all. "I'll call you back," I said.

I turned on my TV and checked the "adult" pay-per-view channels. Sure enough, there it was, exactly as my brother had said. The next showing wasn't for another hour but I couldn't wait that long. I grabbed my keys and ran out to the car.

It's not that I really wanted to watch it. I'd already seen the live show and I was in no hurry to relive the experience. I kind of expected the film to be released without being notified, if only because of what happened to Tim. But I'd anticipated at least one phone call from Brandon to discuss the small matter of my pseudonym. Nobody in porn uses their real name, after all, and I assumed that I'd be given the same courtesy.

As I drove to the nearest video store, I called Brandon on my cellphone.

"Hey, buddy," Brandon purred, "I was hoping to hear from you."

"Somebody said they saw my video," I said, unable to hide the panic in my voice.

"Great," he said cheerfully. "What video?"

"The one you directed. Don't you remember?"

"I'm sorry, sport, I do a lot of videos. You'll have to give me more of a clue."

I gave him a brief synopsis. "Oh yeah," he said. "Good flick. The studio's already talking about a sequel."

Brandon was cut off by a series of crackles and hisses. A few seconds passed and I heard a loud beep. "Sorry," he said. "I'm driving through Coldwater. I lost you there for a moment."

"What name did you use?"

"What name did I use for what?"

"My porn name. I never gave you my porn name."

"Sure, you did," he said. "I have it written down here someplace." I heard the rustling of papers, and then more hissing.

I was certain he was mistaken. I hadn't given him a name because I was still trying to find the perfect one. I wanted something clever but not too brainy. I'd considered using Mario Puzzo (the extra "z" would set me apart from the *Godfather* author) but decided against it for fear of being slapped with a lawsuit.

Maybe it wasn't too late, I told myself. They'd just have to recall any of the videos that'd already been shipped to the stores. It would be a little expensive but a major mistake had been made and it needed to be corrected.

"—And I'm pretty sure that's what you told me," Brandon said, returning mid-sentence.

I needed a pseudonym fast, while I still had Brandon on the phone. I tried to remember that old party game, something about combining the name of your first pet with the street you grew up on.

"Freckles Madison!" I screamed.

"What?" Brandon asked.

"Freckles Madison! Freckles Madison! For the love of God, Freckles Madison!"

"You're breaking up again. Listen, I'm gonna hang up, but I'll try to... Bzzwppt... and we'll make sure you... zzzfpt..."

Brandon's voice dissolved into static and then he was gone.

I arrived at the video store and raced back to the adult section. They had a large selection and none of it was alphabetized. It was like finding a needle in a haystack. I began pulling out videos at random, muttering softly to myself.

"Where are you?" I wheezed. "You can't hide from me

forever."

After making a complete mess and scaring away most of the other customers, I finally found it. I studied the box, scanning for any trace of my name. Satisfied that I had been spared at least one humiliation, I took my video to the front counter.

"How's that porn revolution coming along?" the store's employee asked with a smirk. I said nothing and hurriedly threw him some wrinkled bills.

I returned home, found that my wife was still gone, and skulked into the living room. I shoved the video into our VCR and stood there until I saw the title splash onto the screen. I limply collapsed onto the couch, unable to look away.

Watching the finished product of so many weeks (okay, *hours*) of tireless effort brought out mixed emotions. There were moments when I felt genuinely proud of what I'd accomplished. I had a produced screenplay, which was more than half the writers in Hollywood could say. It wasn't art, sure, but it was permanent or at least as permanent as celluloid could be.

My occasional surges of pride were quickly snuffed out by the haunting realization that I had contributed to something so rotten that it was almost unwatchable. It was drivel. Worse than drivel, it was crap, pure and simple. I suppose a lot could be explained by the acting. The performances were absolutely awful, even worse than I remembered. The actors garbled their lines so badly, it almost seemed that the entire cast was suffering from the same disabling speech impediment. But I knew that I had to share at least some of the blame.

My dialogue was stilted and forced, and none of it was as funny as I'd once envisioned. I tried to tell myself that I'd intended it this way. It was all part of my plan to create the perfect porn parody. But deep down, I knew that I hadn't been quite so cunning. Every painful line, every inane plot point, every porn cliché, it was all bleached of irony. However good my intentions might have been in the beginning, somewhere along the way, whether out of impatience or just plain laziness, I had inadvertently written a fairly typical, unremarkable porn film.

After suffering through almost an hour and a half of unimaginable shame, the moment of truth arrived. The closing credits rolled and I didn't have to wait long to find the answer I'd been searching for:

written by
ERIC SPITZNAGEL

Oddly, I felt nothing. Not angry, not panicky. I was dead inside. In a way, I was almost peaceful. The worst had come and I'd survived it just fine. Now all that was left to do was check myself into a YMCA and begin a new life as a bitter recluse. It wouldn't be so bad. If I got bored, I could always move into the sewers and live with the mole people. Hell, with these credentials, I could be *king* of the mole people. Who needs a career in the arts when you have an army of sewer dwellers at your command?

My cellphone chirped. I didn't much care who it was. Now that I had stopped caring, nobody could touch me.

It was Brandon. "Sorry about before. I just wanted to call you back and settle this misunderstanding about your pseudonym."

"Don't worry about it," I said.

"It's Spitznagel, right? I'm pretty sure that's what you told me."

"That's my real name."

"It is?"

"Yeah."

He chuckled. "That's wild. I could have sworn it was fake. It just... *sounds* like a porn name."

"I guess."

"So, are you coming to the release party?"

"The what?"

"We rented a club down in Hollywood for tomorrow night. Everybody's going to be there. And it's in your honor, buddy. You're the man of the hour."

A miserable laugh escaped from my lips. "Sure," I said, "I'll be there." Why not? At this point, I had nothing to lose.

7

The woman staring back at me was beautiful, in a creepy Fembot sort of way. She had a thick mane of sculpted blonde hair, flawless olive skin, and breasts like two perfect geometric circles. She leered seductively but there was something insincere about her expression. Her sexuality was so false, so utterly disingenuous, that I couldn't help but feel just a little dirty by my own arousal.

I don't know how long I stood there gazing at her before I realized that she was just a photograph. Floating above her breasts — those mesmerizing breasts — was the title of my porno, spelled out in huge silver letters meant to look futuristic. I read it a few times, not entirely believing it. This wasn't my film, I thought. It couldn't be. For one thing, I didn't recognize the model. I still remembered every excruciating moment from my day at the porno set and I was almost positive that she wasn't in the cast.

But the more I looked at her, the more I doubted my own memory. I'd met maybe half a dozen actresses over the last few weeks and I was still having difficulty telling them apart. After awhile, the constant barrage of blonde hair and fake boobs began to blend together and everybody looked the same. I studied her face for some recognizable feature, a mole or unplucked eyebrow hair or any slight imperfection that might differentiate her from all the others. Nothing. She was just another cookie cutout of bland sexuality.

"Can we go inside now?" my wife asked, tugging at my sleeve.

We were standing outside a nightclub on Sunset Boulevard, just a stone's throw away from the Viper Room and Whisky A-Go-Go. Despite its location, this place had none of the notoriety of its more famous neighbors. And that may have been why Brandon chose it for our release party. With no history or regular celebrity clientele to speak of, this club was pure Hollywood Lite. Not as glamorous or elegant as the real thing, but available at a steep discount.

"How much do you think that cost?" I asked my wife, pointing at the poster. It was stapled to the club's front door, the only indication that a film premiere gala was taking place inside.

"I don't know," she said. "What does it matter?"

It mattered a lot, actually. At least to me. I went into this business anticipating low production values. And for the most part, that's exactly what I got. My video looked like a public access cable TV show on a bad day. But this poster stood in stark contrast to porn's usual tendency towards under-financing. The vibrant colors, the expert layout, the meticulous attention to detail. This wasn't another hack job. It was a professional work of promotional art, worthy of any major Hollywood studio. I couldn't be sure, but it seemed like at least half of our production budget had been spent on a 27 by 40-inch piece of paper.

I should have expected as much from an industry that was, after all, a joke. I guess I had hoped that eventually the joke would end. But the gags just kept right on coming with no end in sight. Certainly there had to be a punchline eventually.

"Can we go inside now?" my wife asked again, growing impatient. "I want to get this over with."

I wasn't buying any of it. I knew she wanted to be here considerably more than I did. When I'd told her about this party, she begrudgingly insisted on coming along though I never asked. She claimed that she just wanted to keep an eye on me, but I knew better. She was lonely. She'd spent much of the last year socializing almost exclusively with game show contestants. (Her game show winnings were still, sadly, our only dependable source of income.) Not that she actually believed she could find more meaningful friendships within the porn world. I think she only wanted to have at least one conversation that didn't involve trivia.

We pushed open the door, walked inside, and almost instantly my stomach muscles clenched up in horror. It was an onslaught of stimulus coming from all directions. There were flashing strobe lights designed to cause a seizure, blaring techno music that was rapidly pounding my brain into soft oatmeal. I tried to breathe but was overcome with the pungent odor of fresh peroxide and day-old perfume. And then I began coughing from the smoke. Not cigarette smoke but that machine-generated fake stage smoke preferred by glam rock bands. All in all, it wasn't far from how I'd imagined Hell.

I must have been the only one who felt this way because the place was packed. The crowd, standing shoulder to shoulder, was a veritable cross-section of sexual dysfunction. Some were porn professionals, others just sex enthusiasts. But they all loudly advertised their sexual preferences with every skin-tight outfit, every pierced appendage, every jiggle of barely concealed private parts. These were people for whom the term "missionary position" had long since lost all meaning. It was doubtful that any of them had ever performed a sexual act that didn't in some way involve a trapeze.

I turned to my wife who couldn't have looked more shaken if we'd stumbled into a room full of talking monkeys. We said nothing, just stood there and stared as countless impossibly thin women paraded past us, their breasts strangely motionless. I'd seen plenty of surgically enhanced breasts before but never in such large numbers. I wondered if these women even remembered what it was like to have natural breasts, when the laws of physics still applied to them.

"Spitznagel! You ugly son of a bitch! Get your ass over here!"

I squinted through the haze of smoke, trying to see who was yelling. A figure emerged, coming into view, and for a moment it almost looked like... a cowboy. His spurs clinked against the floor as he approached and I could make out the silhouette of a ten-gallon hat bobbing drunkenly, almost in sync with the music. When the smoke finally cleared, I could see that it was Ray dressed from head to toe in a leather cowboy outfit, complete with huge belt buckle, holsters, and chaps adorned with tiny rhinestones.

"Good to see you, old man," he slurred, slapping me roughly on the back. "What the hell are you doing here? Wanted to see how the other half lives?"

He laughed at this, coarse laughter that made it sound like he was gargling gravel. He pulled me closer, clenching the back of my neck. His eyes were glassy and out of focus, and his breath smelled minty. It was obvious that he had already enjoyed his fair share of cocktails and any number of narcotics.

Just over his shoulder, I saw a woman standing behind him. She was wearing silver hot pants and a matching tank top which fit her so snugly that it left very little to the imagination. I was particularly alarmed by her camel toe, outlined in perfect gynecological detail, its sharp edges giving the appearance of a concealed weapon. Her breasts were, of course, enormous. But they seemed almost fragile, as if at any moment they might crumble and disintegrate.

Ray turned to see who I was looking at and quickly stumbled towards the woman, placing an arm around her. He leaned his entire body weight against her like a drunk clutching a parking meter for support.

"I'd like you to meet my future ex-wife," he announced. The laughter again. The horrible, horrible laughter. "This is Ginger," he continued. "We just signed her yesterday."

I made a quick check for prosthetic limbs but all her parts seemed to be her own. Ray clicked his tongue lewdly and turned to wink at me.

"What do you think? Check out the bod on this chick. Fucking hot, right? You're sporting wood as we speak, am I right?" He slapped my hand like he thought I might reach for her. "Back away from the merchandise, fuckhead."

He circled her, admiring every curve with bloodshot eyes, inviting me to do the same. The woman didn't protest, just waited patiently. She was apparently accustomed to being put on display by lecherous, intoxicated men. While it didn't bother her, she could not have looked more bored. It was an expression I've seen mostly on convenience store clerks as they counted the minutes until their shift was over and they could go home.

I tried to make eye contact with her, give her some indication that I knew how humiliating this was and assure her that I wasn't like all the others. She wouldn't return my gaze. It felt like she was looking right through me. But then her eyes narrowed, her face crinkled as she studied me more closely. And then came a flicker of recognition. I assumed she had confused me with somebody else. An old boyfriend maybe? Or a drug contact? Who knows?

"Nice to see you again," she said with a half-smile. "Felipe, isn't it?"

Instantly I remembered where we'd met before and the clumsy lie that had been my mortifying first encounter with an actual porn actress. It was a moment I'd managed to block out of my mind, feeling somewhat assured that I'd never have to see her again. I wanted to kick myself. I should have seen her coming, should have recognized her as soon as Ray had introduced us. But how was I to know? There's got to be thirty, forty women in this industry named Ginger.

Thankfully, Ray was either too drunk to notice or too drunk to care. "You gotta see this," he said, then turned to Ginger. "Do that thing you showed me."

She sighed, sneering to acknowledge that I had somehow escaped the public ridicule I so richly deserved. She lowered herself to the floor, resting her back against the sticky surface, and raised her legs into the air. She pulled them back, further than should have been humanly possible, finally resting both feet against the back of her neck.

Ray giggled maniacally, delighted by her feat of elastic gymnastics. I couldn't share his enthusiasm. It made me nauseous. I couldn't bear to look at her, and yet I couldn't look away. She glared from behind her taut legs, the fishnet stockings beginning to rip from the pressure. 'I didn't ask for this,' I wanted to tell her. 'I didn't ask to witness this bizarre freak show act. You've got the wrong guy.'

"Is that not fucking fantastic?" Ray yelled, clapping his hands like a child at Disney World. I just nodded. "Wait," he said. "It just gets better." He looked around the room, searching for something. "You think this club has a fire extinguisher?"

"I'm out of here," I heard a voice say. My wife pushed past me, heading straight for the bar. I had completely forgotten that she was there. She'd been standing next to me the whole time, had said nothing, probably waiting for an introduction. I called out for her, begged her to wait, but she disappeared into the crowd. I tried to follow but a hand pulled me back.

"I hear you've been getting offers," Ray said, his voice suddenly low and menacing.

"What?"

"From other studios. Word's out that you've got heat. There's interest."

"I haven't gotten any offers."

"Hey, don't worry about it. I understand completely. Don't want to say anything until the ink is dry, right?"

"No, I—" My head swiveled toward the bar, hoping to catch a glimpse of my wife.

"I don't blame you. You're a big-time writer now. Can't be blamed for wetting your beak a little." Ray leaned in a little too close. "I just want you to remember that we had a deal. You're going to finish that script you promised me. That's your number one priority."

"Well, sure." Where the hell did my wife go?

"If I find out that you're walking out on us because someone made you a better offer, I will *not* be a happy man."

"I'm not walking out," I assured him.

"Just because I didn't make you sign a contract doesn't mean we don't have a deal. I gave you a chance when you were nothing, when you were just some punk kid with a laptop. Don't you forget that," Ray hissed.

"I would never—" Crap. It's just too damn crowded in here to even see the bar.

"You know, there's such a thing as loyalty. But I suppose that means nothing to a guy like you."

"I'm telling you," I insisted, "I haven't gotten any offers."

"Listen to me! Listen to me, goddammit!" Ray yelled, spraying me with a fine mist of spit. "You fucking fuck me and I promise you, you will rue the day! You will rue the fucking day! Do you hear me?"

"I hear you."

"I will cut out your still beating heart and eat it right in front of you. I will fuck your fucking corpse. Make hot sweaty love to your fucking skull." His eyes were bulging. "I am *not* kidding."

"I'm sure that you're not."

"I know people. *Bad* people. You get what I'm saying?"

Visions of John Holmes and the Wonderland Murders flashed through my head. This had the potential to get very ugly and there was no way I could get out of it now. I was going to become one of Ray's loyal writer minions or I would wind up dead. It was as simple as that.

"I swear to you, I am not walking out. I'm finishing your script, and if you want, I'll write as many scripts as you need. Honestly, that is truth."

He looked at me, trying to decide whether he could trust

me. And then, slowly, he released his grip on my shirt.

"Okay," he said gently, patting my cheek. "That's all I wanted to know. Go get a drink. This is a party, boy. Have some fun."

I scurried away, scanning the club for my wife. She was the only one in this place not dressed for S&M, how difficult could she be to spot? I walked towards the bar, pushing my way into the throng of revelers. I struggled against them at first, but the crowd was too thick with bodies. I was being tossed and turned like a rag doll. Rather than fight, I swam with the current, hoping it would spit me out eventually.

Before long, I was just a few feet away from the bar. I could see it, could almost reach out and touch it. But there was too much flesh pressed against me. I might have been able to jam an elbow into a few ribs and break free but it wouldn't have done much good. Standing directly in my path were two women in matching leather catsuits. They might have noticed and gotten out of my way, had they not been preoccupied with kissing.

This wasn't a friendly kiss either. This was a full-on, hips-grinding, hands-groping, spit-trickling-down-the-chin *kiss*. Their tongues were locked in battle, slapping, thrusting, struggling for dominance. Their mouths were so full of piercings, I could hear a sharp metallic clicking as their tongue studs thumped against each other.

I was fascinated, sure. Who wouldn't be at least a little intrigued? But I averted my eyes. I did this for a variety of reasons. First, I was sure that if I did look, wide-eyed and slobbering, that would be the very moment my wife would show up. I knew enough about comedic structure not to walk into such an obvious set-up.

But probably the main reason I didn't look was my innate understanding of my own body's chemistry. Two gorgeous lesbians embracing like greased weasels was just the sort of eye candy that could trigger an unfortunate display of male appreciation. It would have been biologically impossible *not* to become aroused. And when nature took its course — given my close proximity to the entangled lovers — there was no way I could avoid... saying hello, if you will. No, that wouldn't be good. The police would have to become involved, charges would be filed, and all because I lost my wife in a crowd of horny porn stars.

Suddenly, the slurping stopped. Maybe they left, I thought. Moved on to somewhere more private. I turned my gaze for a quick peek and saw that both women were now staring at me.

I wasn't sure what to do. They didn't move, didn't seem particularly disturbed that a strange man was standing just inches away, watching them kiss. I gave them one of those "Wow, isn't this embarrassing? For both of us, I mean" grimaces. I thought this would be enough for them to get the picture. If they would just step aside, I could get to the bar and this whole unfortunate business would be behind us.

"You got twenty dollars?" one of the women asked.

"Uh... no," I said.

"Then fuck off."

They resumed kissing, and it looked like I may be stuck there indefinitely. But then the crowd shifted ever so slightly, just enough for me to squeeze through and find a sliver of available space next to the bar.

My wife was still nowhere to be found and I wasn't eager to return to the black hole of the dance floor just yet. I decided to stay put, let her find me, maybe have a quick drink or two. I signaled to the bartender, a bald man with a tattoo that covered most of his skull, but he ignored me.

"Hey, Chico," a bearded man next to me yelled. "Can we get a little service down here?"

The bartender flashed a smile of gold teeth and walked towards us. "Give me a Sheep Dip," the bearded man said. "And one for my friend here."

I didn't realize that the "friend" he was referring to was me until I felt a hand on my shoulder and turned to see the bearded man grinning. His eyes were hidden behind blue-tinted John Lennon sunglasses and he wore a blazer with some sort of insignia emblazoned on the breast pocket. He seemed out of place in this environment, more suited to a yacht club potluck than this seedy gathering.

The bartender grabbed a rusty, unmarked bottle filled with a tan liquid and poured two shots. I picked up my glass and examined its contents.

"What is this?" I asked.

"Scotch," the bearded man said. "It's pretty good stuff. Just try not to think of the name."

The bearded man downed his drink in one gulp, then slammed the glass back on the bar for a refill. I took a quick sip, and after waiting to be sure that I wouldn't go blind, finished the rest.

"So you're a writer," the man said matter-of-factly, before throwing back his second shot.

"How could you tell?" I asked, surprised that it was so obvious.

He tapped a finger against his forehead. "Simple process of elimination," he said. "You're not dressed like a whore, so you're probably not an actor. You don't have an underage girl on your arm, so it's a safe bet that you're not a producer. And you haven't yet called me a cocksucker or made some irrational, unrealistic demand of me, so you can't be a director. That means that you're either lost and terribly misinformed about what kind of nightclub this is, or you're a writer."

He extended his hand. "I'm a writer too," he said. "Dick Longfellow, *Sluts In Heat Part Three*."

I didn't remember asking him for his credits but I assumed that he expected me to do the same. I shook his hand, announcing my name and the title of my movie. He laughed at this, like we had just shared a private joke.

"Nice pen-name," he said. "Very subtle. I like it."

With formal introductions out of the way, we had nothing further to talk about. We just sat in silence, surrounded by the roar of the party, fingering our empty glasses, occasionally nodding our heads at nothing in particular.

After finishing his third shot, Dick stood up from his barstool. I thought for a moment that this would be the end of it. We would say our goodbyes, wish each other luck, and go our separate ways. But he had other plans for me.

"There's some people I'd like you to meet," he said.

8

It's often been said that high school imitates life. Not the good stuff either, but the unfair social hierarchies that gave adolescence that extra special sting. It was supposed to have ended after graduation but, as it turned out, the whole miserable experience was just a microcosm of the adult world. The band geeks of yesterday can't ever totally escape those cultural roles and once you've been assigned to the "uncool" table in the cafeteria, you're pretty much stuck there for life.

I was reminded of that fact as I looked around at all the bitter, alienated faces. Just a few feet away, the beautiful people were dancing, flirting, enjoying the time of their lives. But we were huddled in the corner, watching the party with jealous eyes. Though we would have liked to believe otherwise, we were the cultural equivalent of the chess club.

"So the director tells me, 'We're going with a different approach.' Like I don't know what *that* means."

"Gonzo, right?"

"Isn't it always?"

"You'd think they'd learn. Actors should not be allowed to improvise."

We were standing near the bathroom, which may have been why we were left alone. Hardly anybody was drinking (besides us, at least) and, as most of the drugs were being consumed out in the open, there was no good reason for anybody to visit the restroom. Except maybe for sex. But judging from the groans coming from the crowd, they were just a few more snorts of coke away from a full-blown group grope.

By all accounts, I should have been a mess. My wife was still missing. I'd had one too many shots of Sheep Dip. And as the hours dragged on, the club was rapidly filling up and the new arrivals looked dangerous. The sort of people who still had fond memories of Altamont. But I was totally relaxed. Not a worry in the world. It'd been too long since I'd been surrounded by other writers. These were my people. My blood. I belonged with them. If things turned ugly, they would protect me. I was sure of it.

"I hate gonzos too, but I understand them. Half the contract girls can barely read. They need their dialogue to be spelled out phonetically."

"The tits get bigger, the brain gets smaller."

"If you ask me, there should be standardized testing for porn stars. Something to weed out the mentally impaired."

"Are you kidding? There'd be nobody left. We'd have to start casting sock puppets."

When Richard (he never told me to call him Richard, but I wasn't about to use "Dick" or "Mr. Longfellow") dragged me over to meet his friends, I was prepared for the worst. But these people — all porn writers — weren't that much different from any other literary professional. All the standard personality types were represented here, all the staples of the writing clique. There was the single mom, the unshaven chain-smoker, the vaguely effeminate blonde boy, the Kevin Smith wanna-be in a trenchcoat and baseball cap worn backwards.

Despite their self-imposed exile to the sidelines, this was no island of misfit toys. During our introductions, each writer had told me their name and then rattled off a laundry list of professional credits (a curious greeting ritual, but one that I was beginning to appreciate). Most of them had been working writers long before they got into porn. Their collective resumés were enough to make me salivate with envy. Movies, TV, Off-Broadway. A few had even written for *The Simpsons*, the Holy Grail among writers. They hadn't ended up in porn for lack of better options. They had *chosen* this career. They *wanted* to be here.

"This gonzo trend is just the tip of the iceberg. We're entering a whole new era of interactive media."

"I was thinking the same thing. Have you seen what they've got on the Internet these days? Streaming video, live feeds... where's it all going to end?"

"Personally, I blame DVDs. You let the audience pick their own camera angles, pretty soon they're running the show. We're completely cut out of the process."

"Well, get used to it. Things aren't going to get any better. There's just not a market for fast forwards anymore."

"I hate to admit it, but I think he's right."

"All this new technology makes it less necessary for them to hire writers. We're being systematically eliminated. It's only a matter of time before we're replaced with gigabytes. In another five years, I guarantee you that very few of us will still be working. The entire industry will be run by computer programmers."

I wanted to be sympathetic. I really did. Far be it for me to question any writer's sense of impending doom. I certainly understood what it was like to have an inherent distrust of employers. And I knew that talking about it with other writers only fuels the fire. We have a tendency to reinforce our pessimism, feed off each other's suspicions that the world is against us. To some extent, the paranoia is justified. Most writers can expect to be fucked over at least once in their life. It's just a matter of when and how.

But I couldn't fathom why they were getting so worked up. It's not like we were up against insurmountable odds. If they truly believed that our futures were in jeopardy, we didn't have to take it lying down. I mean, if it were really Us against Them, then surely we would win. We had written for *Futurama* and *National Lampoon* and been to Sundance and taken meetings with Ben Stiller. They didn't understand a world more complex than *Anal Adventures Volumes One to Sixteen.* They were the Goliath to our David and with a few slights of hand that ugly bastard would fall right on his fat ass.

"Have you seen what they're doing with digital technology? It's frightening."

"I was at the trade show in Las Vegas last week and they were already promoting a fully functional cybersex bodysuit."

"My God, it's so Orwellian."

"I'm telling you, the minute it becomes affordable for people to attach electrodes to their genitals, you're going to see video rentals drop to an all-time low."

"It was bound to happen eventually. Tomorrow's porn won't be sold in video stores. It'll be sold at Radio Shack."

"I don't believe that," I said.

All eyes were upon me, disbelieving. The new kid had spoken out of turn. Although they'd instantly accepted me into their group, I doubt any of them had expected me to bully my way into the conversation quite so quickly. But I couldn't let this moment slip away without comment.

"They've been predicting the death of the written word for centuries," I continued. "If we're so afraid of losing our audience, we just have to write smarter scripts."

It was, I thought, am amazingly insightful observation. How brave to have stated that. How bold. I'd stared unblinking into the blackness and found hope. I waited for them to stand up and start applauding, maybe pick me up and carry me around the room on their shoulders. Who wouldn't be inspired to action by such a stirring declaration of solidarity?

But they laughed. They slapped their knees. They found it all terribly amusing.

"That is so sweet," the mother chuckled, caressing my cheek. "You really believe that, don't you?"

"What?" I was incredulous. "You're telling me I'm wrong?"

"You *are* wrong."

"Well, explain to me why."

Richard cleared his throat, searching for the right words. "Post mortem erections," he said. The others nodded in agreement.

"What does that mean?"

"When a body dies, it's capable of an erection for up to three hours afterwards. This is a biological fact. The dead brain tissue doesn't make a bit of difference. It has nothing to do with cerebral activity. It's just an instinctual response, a knee-jerk reaction. You see what I'm saying?

"No, I don't," I replied.

"A cock doesn't need to think."

I wanted to protest, but how could I? He'd brilliantly brought all my pretensions crashing down with one well-placed corpse metaphor. It's one thing to be made a fool of by a civilian but when a fellow writer publicly ridicules you, the effect is always more devastating. I'd been betrayed by one of my own.

"We know how it is," the Kevin Smith wannabe said. "We all started out in this business thinking we could change it. For years, I was convinced that my dialogue could compete with the sex. It was funnier, more original, and a hell of a lot sexier. I honestly believed that people were jerking off to my words. But it doesn't happen that way."

"They don't call it the 'fast forward' to be cute," Richard said. "It's the reality and the sooner you realize that, the better off you'll be."

"But, then, why bother?" I said. "If it's just crap, and it'll always be crap, then why do it?"

"Because it's a sweet gig."

"But it's *porn*. You can do better. You've *done* better. You're telling me that this is more satisfying than writing for television or film?"

"You have to understand something." It was the cigarette guy's turn to speak. "Working for a TV show is no picnic. There are constant demands on you to be clever. It's unrelenting. Most TV writers get bleeding ulcers within their first year."

"Movies are no better," another writer added. "The pressure for quality has gotten ridiculous. Studios don't just want box office hits anymore. They want critical raves, Oscar nominations. Nobody can produce at that level all the time. It's too exhausting."

"The expectations in porno are just more reasonable," said

Richard. "If you deliver something halfway decent, they're ecstatic. But give them something above average and they flip out. They think you're a genius and the money never stops pouring in."

"Think of it this way. If they're stupid enough to pay us for doing nothing, we'd be idiots not to take the money and run."

They continued pushing the argument but after awhile I stopped listening. My heart was broken. In hindsight, I would have preferred if they had turned out to be hacks. At least hacks don't know any better. But these were talented writers, writers who had done great things once, been given opportunities that most only dream about, and they had just decided to stop caring. Whatever aspirations or artistic credibility they once had had been abandoned long ago and they'd settled for a cozy existence of low expectations. They might as well have gone into advertising. There really was no difference anymore. They were just spewing out an endless torrent of formulaic crap, waiting for that fat paycheck that would help them forgot all those silly dreams of creative relevance.

I had gotten it all wrong. Porn wasn't a rite of passage for young writers, a means to hone their chops while they waited for bigger and better things. For some of them, sure, that may have been the case. But there was also a very real danger of porn becoming a final destination. You start out strong, set your goals high, struggle for as long as you can. Maybe you even achieve some modicum of success. But when things get too complicated and you realize that you don't have the energy or desire anymore to keep fighting for a career, porn will be there to offer an easy way out. You're still technically a writer. And a *paid* writer, no less. How many people can say that? But the sad truth is, porn was a safety net, and you jumped too soon.

They kept right on talking, complaining about something or other. Technology would be the death of porno, jobs would be lost... blah, blah, blah. I suppose I should have joined in their cries of protest, should have mourned the impending drying out of the porn gravy train. But I couldn't bring myself to care. It just didn't seem like we would be losing anything of real importance.

I don't know how long I stood there pretending to listen, pretending to be one of them, before I finally managed to slink away.

A few minutes later, I was running for the exit. Not that I was in any immediate danger. I just needed to get out of there before I became consumed with claustrophobic panic. Maybe it was the rapidly expanding crowd, bodies piled upon bodies, far exceeding the legal limit. Maybe it was the club's walls which were covered in red velvet padding, giving it all the cozy ambiance of an insane asylum rec room. Whatever the reason, I had to leave immediately, if only to assure myself that escape was still possible.

Out in the parking lot, the Santa Ana winds were gusting hard. The desert breeze had rolled in, bringing with it a mini dust storm. The air had the brownish color of exhaust and it was difficult to breathe without wheezing. Surprisingly, there were easily half as many people out here as inside the club. They were laughing, dancing, snorting coke off the hoods of cars. Condoms had been blown up like balloons and attached to antennas, adding to the party atmosphere. It was like a tailgate party for perverts.

Girl, you looks good
Won't you back that ass up

You's a fine motherfucker
Won't you back that ass up

Music was being pumped through speakers attached to the club's roof. Apparently the owners were well aware that their patrons were spilling out into the parking lot and had decided to play along rather than fight against it. I hadn't really listened before but I was beginning to notice a pattern in their choice of songs. Iggy Pop's *Butt Town*, Beastie Boys' *Shake Your Rump*, Tragically Hip's *Butts Wigglin'*, Sir Mix-A-Lot's *Baby Got Back*. They were all songs about butts. Was this just a coincidence or an intentional theme?

I wandered through the parking lot, looking for my car. It seemed like as good a place as any to wait for my wife. I also wanted to make sure that nobody was using it for their own devious purposes. Would cocaine leave a stain? I had no idea. But that was the least of my worries. If I found ass prints on the hood, I'd just have to sell it. I couldn't drive around in a car knowing that some stranger's naked flesh had been pressed up against it.

I weaved through the crowd, careful not to brush against anybody. I'd had too much bad touching for one night. I needed a shower immediately, just to be on the safe side. Under the harsh lights of the parking lot, I had a better view of the women and their lopsided bodies. I spotted a few scars, just under their breasts, which I assumed were from implant surgery. But they might have been liposuction scars. Maybe both. It was shocking that any of these women had the energy to stand up anymore, with so many fluids being pumped in and out of their bodies with such regularity. How did they justify butchering themselves like that? I suppose it's just a matter of perspective. All that surgery hadn't really changed their body weight, just... shifted it a little. The amount of fat sucked out of them was probably in direct proportion to the amount of implants put in. If you look at it that way, pound for pound, it all evened out in the end.

I found my car and, after examining it for blemishes, leaned against the driver's side door, keys in hand, ready to jump inside and turn the ignition at the first sign of my wife. Over the speakers, another butt song was being played.

Shake ya ass
Watch ya self
Shake ya ass
Show me what you workin' wit

My body swayed to the music as I hummed along. It helped calm my shattered nerves. In the distance, I could see a man approaching. He was wearing a jacket covered in red feathers and he was heading right for me. I turned my head, focused on my singing, hoping he'd just pass by if I didn't make eye contact. I tightened my grip on the keys, ready to use them like a switchblade if I had to. I hoped it wouldn't come to that but I was ready for anything.

"Leaving so soon, sport?"

I immediately relaxed. It was just Brandon. I turned and smiled, trying to appear casual. "No, no, course not," I said in a lazy drawl. "I'm just... hanging out. Enjoying the view."

He cocked his head as a gaggle of women passed us, their breasts suspended in the air like hovercrafts. "And what a view it is, huh?" he said with a wink.

He leaned next to me on the car and ran a thumb across the bridge of his nose, cleaning it, wiping away the evidence. He looked at me again and something in my expression seemed to concern him. "What's on your mind?" he asked.

"Nothing. Why?"

"You look upset."

I shrugged. "No, not really. I'm fine."

"Wait, let me guess." He thought for a minute, giving his nose one last swab. "You can't decide whether to keep writing for Ray or take one of those offers you've been getting."

"What offers? I haven't been getting any offers. Why does everybody think that?"

"Well, you'll be getting offers soon enough. You've got heat. Wait a few days and every studio in town will be begging to work with you."

"I really don't think so."

"Whatever. You'll see. You shouldn't be wasting your talents on Ray anyway. You're better than that. I mean, I love the guy. I really do. But he's a freak. Did you know that last year he directed eight movies about clowns?"

"No, I—"

"Exactly. It makes no sense. Clowns are not sexy. Clowns are scary. Have you ever seen a clown having sex?"

"No." Thankfully, that was the truth.

"It's profoundly disturbing. All that giggling and nose honking, not to mention the big shoes. It's a real turn-off. If there's one rule to making a good porno, it's that you should never, *ever* remind your audience of John Wayne Gacy."

"That's good advice."

"I tried to tell him that but Ray wouldn't listen. He was convinced he could pull it off. Even when the movies bombed, he kept insisting there was a market. You don't want to be in business with a guy like that. You should be making big films, *important* films. Not that arty-farty shit."

"Point taken."

"Unless that's what you want. I'm not trying to tell you how to run your career. Maybe clowns turn you on, I don't know. I'm not going to judge you. I'm just saying, it's not for me."

"I can appreciate that." I yawned, stretching my arms for extra effect. I wasn't really tired, I just wanted to leave this place. I could stay here and wait, but who knows how long my wife would take to find me? Or, better idea, I could get in the car and drive around the block a few hundred times, however long it took. Eventually I'd see her, hit the horn until I got her attention, and we'd be off. She might be upset that I'd left her there but surely she could appreciate the need for a quick getaway.

"There's something else bothering you, isn't there?" Brandon asked.

I slouched against the car, resting an arm on the roof like I had every intention of staying here indefinitely. "I'm fine, really."

Brandon nodded, like he understood something that I had yet to grasp. "Were you aware that the majority of porn actors don't die from sexually transmitted diseases?" he inquired.

I wasn't sure how to respond. It was apropos of nothing. I started to speak but could manage only a few facial tics.

"Is that a fact?" I finally said.

"Most people think it's AIDS but that's a fallacy. The number one cause of death among porn stars is self-inflicted gunshot wounds."

"I had no idea."

"It's true. Just look at the body count. Wendy Williams, Cal Jammer, Megan Leigh, Shauna Grant, Savannah. They all offed themselves with shotguns. You know what the second most common cause of death is?"

"Uh..."

"Asphyxiation. Followed closely by overdose-related suicides. And *then* AIDS. It's weird, huh? Everybody thinks that this industry needs condoms but what it really needs is more therapy."

We both shook our heads, marveling at the strangeness of it all. I knew that he was trying to make me feel better but all this talk of dead porn stars was just making me more depressed.

"I've been in this business for almost ten years," he continued. "I've seen a lot of friends die, watched a lot of my peers take the easy way out. But I've never worried that it could happen to me. I'm just not the depressive sort. I've never been sad for no reason, never been plagued with self-doubt, never once had suicidal thoughts. And you know why that is?"

"Uh..."

"I want to show you something." He reached into his pocket and pulled out a wallet. He flipped it open to the inner sleeve, the part usually intended for family photos. He pointed to a picture and I had to look more closely to see what it was. It seemed to be an angel covered in gold body paint. But upon closer inspection, it turned out to be a small statue.

"That's an Adult Video News Award," he told me. "This may not mean much to you, but believe me, it's the most honest honor we can get in this industry. They don't just give these to anybody. You have to prove yourself. You have to demonstrate that you're at the top of your field."

"That's great, Brandon. Good for you."

Well, what was I supposed to say? He was obviously waiting for a reaction. He had that look in his eyes, that expectant gaze you usually see in parents when they're showing you baby photos. I could have mocked him, could have come right out and said,

"How adorable, it looks just like you." But I couldn't bring myself to be that cruel. Apparently he saw nothing unusual about carrying around a photo of an award statue in his wallet. And that was probably for the best. If he suspected even for a moment just how pathetic it was, that depression he'd been avoiding for so many years might finally catch up with him.

"When I get up in the morning, I can look in the mirror with a sense of pride. I'm not ashamed of what I do. Sure, sometimes it's bad. Sometimes it's *really* bad. But of all the people who do it, I do it the best. You see what I'm saying? I'm the *best*."

"That's a nice way to look at it."

"It's the only way, sport. If you compare yourself with the greats of cinema, sure, you're going to feel inadequate. But you have to examine your life in the right context."

"And what would that be?"

"We may be at the bottom, but we're at the *top* of the bottom."

In a twisted sort of way, this made perfect sense. And he really believed it, that's what made it so beautiful. I wanted more than anything to be like him, to be so blissfully unaware, to see the world through his blinders. All around him was evidence that he was wrong, tangible proof that his life was a joke, but he wouldn't look at it, wouldn't acknowledge its presence.

"You know what might help?" Brandon said. "If you ever find yourself feeling low, and you think that everything you've written is terrible and it's all been a big waste of time, I want you to remember one simple thing."

"What's that?"

He spoke softly, enunciating each word. "It's not my fault, it's theirs."

"Whose fault?"

"Everybody: the actors, the producers, the audience and their filthy, stupid desires. There's always somebody out there to muck it up for you. But there's nothing you can do about that. Say it with me. It's not my fault, it's theirs."

"I'd really rather—"

"Just say it." He lifted his chin, cueing us to begin. "It's not my fault," we said in unison, "it's theirs."

"There now," he said, beaming. "Don't you feel better?"

I did, actually. And for one brief, fleeting moment, all was right in the world.

9

My wife eventually found her way out of the nightclub, well into the early morning. She wasn't angry that I'd left her there. Quite the opposite. She'd had a great time, she said. Met some fascinating people, had conversations that she could only describe as "Theater of the Absurd." Our evening out had somehow inspired her to write again and the moment we got home, she was back in front of her computer, pounding away at the keys.

I, on the other hand, immediately removed my pants and got into bed. And I stayed there for the next three weeks. I wasn't hiding, I just didn't see any reason to leave the house. Calls came in occasionally, and just as predicted, a few of them were from porn directors asking for scripts, requesting meetings. I ignored them, of course. My wife scolded me for this, said I should get off my ass and take advantage of these opportunities. But I just wasn't interested.

A part of me was curious to see how badly they wanted me. Just how far would they go to sign the hot young porn writer? Would they keep calling? Try to woo me with gifts? What sort of gift would a porn studio consider appropriate? A fruit basket maybe? Or a prostitute? Well, why not? It wasn't outside the realm of possibility. Not that I would have accepted, but still, it would have been nice to know they cared.

When I wasn't loitering around the house in my underwear, I somehow managed to finish another draft of the script for Ray. It was remarkably easy. I talked to Ray on the phone a few times and his notes which once seemed like gibberish were beginning to make more sense. Not that he was getting any better at expressing himself. I had just become quite good at translating his ideas to the page, or at least switching off that part of my brain responsible for logical thought.

There's an essay by David Mamet called "Girl Copy" in which he muses about his early career writing porn captions for *Oui* magazine during the late '70s. "All over the country," he wrote, "adolescent boys and frustrated married men were looking at the sexy photos of the sexy naked women, and these men were having fantasies about them. Here I was, getting twenty grand a year to look at the same photos and create those fantasies, and it felt to me like work."

With all respect to David Mamet, writing porn never seemed like work to me. But I suppose I could understand why a person might think so. When your professional life involves making up sexual fantasies, it can take some of the fun and mystery out of your own fantasy life. The difference was, I never considered what I wrote to be fantasy. Not that it was a reality, at least not for me, but for the actors who would ultimately end up performing my words, it wasn't that far from the truth.

You have to remember, these people aren't like you or me. They're sexual extremists. You don't end up in porn because of a casual interest in sex. You have to be obsessed with it, fanatical in your devotion, driven to push your body to frightening heights of sexual pleasure. What you see on screen is only half the story. Their libidos don't shut down just because the cameras are turned off. They take their work home with them, honing their instruments like classical violinists. And there's very little that they haven't tried or are willing to try. They have sex in city parks, government buildings, barns, public restrooms, planes, furniture stores, cars (parked *and* moving). Any situation they might find themselves in, regardless of how tame or innocuous, could feasibly result in an exchange of bodily fluids.

I'm aware that it sounds like I'm exaggerating. It's natural to assume that because they call themselves actors, what they're doing (or attempting to do) in these movies is acting. But there's a very big difference between what constitutes acting in porn and the conventional definition of acting. When Harrison Ford battles Nazis in *Raiders of the Lost Ark*, we all know that he's just playing an expensive game of make-believe. He's probably never even *met* a Nazi, much less been involved in a high-speed chase with one. But when a porn star plays a role, the line between fiction and truth is a bit more fuzzy.

There's an old story from the porn trenches that may explain my point more clearly. I didn't actually see any of this firsthand but it was told to me by a reliable source and he swears that it happened exactly as he described. According to the story, an actress was doing a scene that involved her seducing a pizza delivery guy. Seconds after the cameras began to roll, she called for the director to cut. She couldn't do it, she said. It was all wrong. The whole premise was too unbelievable. The director asked if she had any suggestions and she told him that the scene could be fixed with a simple costume change. Instead of a Domino's delivery guy, the actor should be dressed as a Pizza Hut delivery guy. "What's the difference?" the director asked. Well, she replied, from her experience, delivery guys from Pizza Hut tended to be hotter and more willing to fuck their female customers.

True story.

So I never thought of myself as a writer of fiction. Rather, I was a journalist, recording the facts as I saw them. Granted, I used my imagination more than most journalists. But I never drew from the well of my own fantasies. When I needed an idea for a script, I simply closed my eyes, made a mental picture of the actress I was writing for and then just pieced together the events of a typical day. Once you knew these people and what made them tick, it was just a matter of thinking like they did. The story was inconsequential. Your characters could be anywhere, doing practically anything. You just had to wait long enough and they would find some reason to have sex.

So writing the script was easy. The real problems started when I *stopped* writing and went back to my normal life. I'd spent so much time concentrating on the sexual lives of porn stars, I forgot that the outside world didn't operate under the same set of rules. Porn had warped my sensibilities and I was having a difficult time readjusting.

I would walk to the store for a pack of cigarettes and be astounded by all the people out on the street who weren't naked. They were everywhere, driving in cars or talking amongst themselves, doing things that didn't in any way involve hardcore sex. And yet they seemed perfectly fulfilled. Who *are* these people? I wondered. How do they live like this?

My wife would occasionally be visited by her female friends, and it was shocking that none of them attempted to mount me. They could carry on entire conversations without being tempted by their sexual impulses, not once reaching out to caress a breast or unbutton a blouse. I was awestruck by their self-control. I wondered if the same thing was happening in other cities. Could it be that all over the world, in millions of homes, there were other people not having sex? It seemed implausible. How did they pass the time? What did they do with their hands?

The neighbors were starting to look at me funny. I could hear them whispering in the halls, avoiding my gaze when I stepped outside to get the mail. Occasionally I would catch children peeking through our window, only to run away shrieking when I advanced on them. I had become the resident crazy hermit. I could imagine what they were saying. "Have you seen the guy who lives in Unit D? I heard he hasn't left his apartment in years. Sometimes, late at night, you can hear him muttering to himself. They say he's mad. *Mad*, I tell you!"

I watched a lot of TV during that period. I hoped it would help but it only made me more confused. I was especially disturbed by sitcoms, which share many of porn's aesthetics. But unlike porn, each contrived set-up led nowhere. Always they went for the laugh, missing countless opportunities for gratuitous sex.

"You fool," I would yell at the television. "Can't you see that she's begging for it? Drop your pants! *Drop your pants!*"

My God, what was wrong with me? Had it really come to this? Had I become one of those twisted old perverts looking for sex in everything? I was a sick man. I needed professional help. I considered checking myself into a detox center. But which one? There were places that treated sex addiction but I was suffering from something more complex than that. Surely there was a clinic in this city that specialized in my unique disorder. A Betty Ford Center for porn professionals. Did such a place even exist? If it did, I couldn't find it in the phone book.

If I was going to kick this thing, shake this monkey off my back, then I would have to do it on my own. I decided to go cold turkey, cut all ties to the porn world. They wouldn't be happy. Ray might even threaten again to have me killed. I'd just have to call his bluff. I might end up with a bullet in my lung but it was a chance I had to take. Better to be dead than live another minute in this hell.

It took me a few days to muster the courage. When I finally made the call, I was relieved that Clark picked up. He would make this easier, or at least wouldn't be so quick to threaten me with bodily harm.

"Eric, thank God it's you. Where've you been? We've been trying to call you all day."

"Listen, I've been doing a lot of thinking, and I don't—"

"We need you to come to the office right away. It's an emergency."

"What kind of emergency?"

"I don't have time to explain now. Just get down here!"

Shit.

Less than an hour later, I was standing between Ray and Clark in a dark, unfurnished room about the size of a walk-in closet. We were looking at their office through a window, one of those one-way mirrors like they have in police interrogation rooms, allowing us to see inside without being detected. It was distressing enough that anybody would have a secret chamber installed in their office but the fact that these men were pornographers added an extra element of creepiness.

"We have to act fast," Ray said. "We can't keep him waiting in there forever."

"Don't worry," Clark said. "Let's just give him some time to think. We don't want to make our move too quickly."

"I still can't believe that he hasn't walked out. I knew that athletes were supposed to be stupid but this is unbelievable."

"Calm down. He's not going anywhere. We've gotten him this far, we're not going to lose him now."

The athlete that Ray and Clark were discussing with excited whispers was sitting in their office, unaware that he was being watched. They didn't have to tell me his name. I recognized him instantly. I wasn't much of a professional basketball fan but I was familiar enough with the NBA to know who I was looking at. He was a megastar, easily in the same league as Michael Jordan or Shaquille O'Neal. I'd seen him play countless times, knew friends and family who idolized him. It didn't seem possible that a celebrity of his magnitude could be here, sitting on that dirty couch, tapping his fingers on his huge knees as he waited for somebody to fetch him.

The story, as it was explained to me, went something like this:

This NBA superstar (let's call him "J.D.") had been partying at an L.A. club when he'd met one of Ray's contract girls. Being recently divorced, he was intrigued by the prospect of sleeping with a real porn actress and eventually ended up back at her apartment. The evening evolved into a weekend and then a full week of sexual Olympics. J.D. surely understood that their relationship would be short-lived, but for the moment at least, he had fallen hard for the girl. Poor J.D. had been seduced by the same siren song that had captivated many a celebrity before him, chief among them Charlie Sheen.

At some point, the actress had suggested to J.D. that he make a guest appearance in one of her videos. Nothing major, just a walk-on role. Maybe a line or two. At first he resisted, but she somehow convinced him that it would be good for his image. He already had a reputation for being the bad boy of basketball. Surely this would only increase his notoriety. Wanting to please her, he agreed, and she sent him to see Ray.

Ray was scarcely able to believe his good fortune but he was also at heart a businessman so he decided to find out if he could negotiate a better deal. "Forget the walk-on role," he'd told J.D. "We want to do something more outrageous. We're working on this new script and you'd be perfect for the lead. There's some nudity involved. Okay, a *lot* of nudity. You'd be having sex in front of the camera. But you're an athlete. You can handle it. Besides," he'd added, "you want notoriety? You want to show the world what you're made of? You can't do much better than this."

It must have been one hell of a sales pitch. When he wanted to, Ray had an uncanny ability to make people forgot common sense and do things that they would never even consider in a more rational state of mind. It was a skill that had served him well. But this was by far his biggest challenge. He'd been preparing for this moment all his life. It was the ultimate test of his ability at coercion, and he'd given it everything he had.

"The cocksucker won't do it," Ray told me, nearly spitting with disappointment. "Said he wants to talk with his agent first. Can you believe that shit?"

As a matter of fact, I could believe that shit. It was a smart move. He understood that he wasn't thinking clearly. He was under the influence of too much sex, and he'd agree to anything just so the fun could continue. His agent would be able to knock some sense into him, get him out of this mess. He hadn't gotten this far in his career by making major business decisions on his own.

Ray was right about one thing. Appearing in a porno would give him notoriety. But would it be the good kind of notoriety, where a mere celebrity was transformed into a cult icon? Or would it be bad notoriety, where one misguided decision would snuff out a career in seconds flat? It could go either way, actually. It's a subject that has been hotly debated among porn scholars. Although no definitive answer has been determined, there's a theory that has yet to be disproved. This theory is better known as the Stallone/Schwartz Principle. Allow me to explain.

Years before *Rocky* made him a household name, Sylvester Stallone got his first major acting role in an obscure 1970 porno called *Party at Kitty and Stud's*. Even by porn standards, it was an awful film with tepid sex scenes and goofy dialogue. ("I'll be velvet-mouthed on your shank of love.") Sly eventually went on to bigger and better things but whoever owned the rights to *Party at Kitty and Stud's* capitalized on Stallone's fame by re-releasing it on video with the title, *The Italian Stallion*. It enjoyed huge sales for a brief period, if only because it contained proof that Stallone was a man of modest endowment (and, interestingly enough, that he had a four-inch scar just under his butt). But public fascination with Stallone's porno past soon quietly faded and today only a few film buffs even remember that it ever existed.

By contrast, we have Scott Schwartz, the child actor who skyrocketed to fame during the early '80s with starring roles in *A Christmas Story* and *The Toy*. Soon after his string of hits, he retired from the business for almost a decade. It wasn't until the mid-'90s that he returned to acting, but the once pudgy-cheeked kid was now all grown up and dropping his pants for the camera. His porn antics in such videos as *Scotty's X-Rated Adventure* and *New Wave Hookers 5* may have proved that Scott wasn't a boy anymore but it didn't exactly help his film career. When he attempted to find work in the mainstream again, he discovered that Hollywood was no longer interested. He had been labeled as damaged goods and there wasn't a studio in town that would touch him.

Two popular actors, both of whom dabbled in porn during their weaker moments. But only one escaped unscathed from the experience while the other continues to be punished. What was the difference, you ask? It was all in the timing. Stallone could claim that he was young, that he had been duped, that he was just another starving actor who needed a quick paycheck. But Schwartz didn't have such a convenient excuse. He had already attained some degree of success, and unless he invested unwisely, he should have had plenty of money left over from his glory years to be financially secure. While Stallone's misdeeds could be written off as a youthful indiscretion — a desperate act by a desperate actor — Schwartz's foray into porn seemed more calculated, a malicious attempt to use his image to make a quick buck.

In other words, pre-celebrity porn is fine. But post-celebrity porn is an altogether different matter. You can make a mistake before you achieve fame. But once you're famous, all bets are off. You should know better.

This NBA player – sorry, *J.D.* – had probably never heard of the Stallone/Schwartz Principle, but I think he understood it intuitively. He was too famous at this point to do something so foolish. He would be crucified by the media, stoned by outraged fans. And worst of all, for the remainder of his professional career, regardless of his accomplishments, he would forever be known as "that basketball player who did a porno."

He would be fine, I told myself. They can't trick him into doing this. As good as Ray was, he wasn't dealing with one of his blonde bimbos anymore. I was almost looking forward to seeing him get shot down.

"We want you to talk to him," Clark said finally.

Come again? "Why me?" I asked.

"You're a writer," Ray said. "You're good with words. We figured that you'd be able to come up with something that'd make him change his mind."

I tried to explain to them that they had misjudged me. Just because a writer knows how to string together a coherent sentence doesn't make him a competent public debater. I could write him a letter, I suggested. Or send a fax to his agent. But they were adamant. I had to speak with him and argue our case. Today. Right now.

"We're not just asking you to do this for us," Ray said. "It's in your best interests to make this happen. This is *your* film we're talking about here."

"Yeah, but—" I protested.

"Can you imagine the publicity?" Clark continued. "It'll be huge. Everybody will be talking about it. We'll have the best-selling video in the country."

"The world!" Ray added.

"You thought the Tommy and Pamela Lee video was a big deal? They've got nothing on us. We're talking millions upon millions of units. Maybe *billions*. Nobody's seen anything like this before."

"I don't know," I said doubtfully. "I just think we should..."

"Listen to me," Ray snarled. "Shut up for a fucking minute and listen. This is not just some stupid porno anymore. We're at a whole different level now."

"I don't think you're grasping the enormity of this thing," Clark implored. "We're asking you to be a part of something bigger than all of us. Something groundbreaking in its scope."

"The fucking *Star Wars* of porn."

"This is our chance to do something important, to create a film that will survive the ages."

"And make a fuckload of money in the process," Ray concluded.

"I just don't want you to regret your decision," Clark said quietly. "Years from now, are you going to think of this moment and feel that you let an opportunity slip away? Or are you going to look back and know that you accomplished something special?"

I was beginning to come around. Actually, at the first mention of how much money we stood to make, I was pretty much sold on the idea. I also suspected that I could get a little more out of this deal than just a healthy bank account. If I played my cards right, I could ride the storm of media exposure all the way to a legitimate writing career. There was nothing particularly special about being a porn writer, but to be the porn writer responsible for the downfall of a great basketball player, well, that might bring me just enough infamy to make a difference.

Oh sure, there were plenty of moral reasons not to do it. It wasn't exactly honorable to cause somebody misfortune for your own financial gain. But I was pretty sure I could live with the guilt. These NBA fuckers had it too good. Their lives were filled with riches and abundant pleasure. Surely they could afford to sacrifice their dignity for the good of one of their fans. After all the times I'd stood in line outside stadiums, waiting to pay two hundred dollars for the privilege of watching a bunch of overpaid college drop-outs put a ball through a hoop, I was *owed* a little payback.

Ray handed over the contract and showed me where J.D. needed to sign. I assured them that everything would be taken care of. I walked through a side door and followed a hallway around to the front entrance of their office. I could hear my heart thumping as I opened the door and walked inside.

J.D. was still sitting on the couch, looking far more nervous than I was. I could tell that he felt vulnerable in this environment. In the NBA, he was considered eccentric. But here, he was out of his element. He was, for perhaps the first time in his life, the normal one.

"How's it going?" I said, casually striding towards him with an outstretched hand.

"Fine," he said, timidly.

He took my hand and shook it. I was shocked at just how enormous he was. I had only ever seen NBA players from a distance or on television. I knew they were big guys but it's an altogether different thing when you meet one in the flesh. Even sitting down, he towered over me.

"I hear you're interested in participating in one of our upcoming projects," I said.

He wrinkled his nose, like he had just caught a whiff of some horrible odor. "I want to think about it," he said.

Don't think about it, I wanted to scream. *Run away. Save yourself. It's too late for me. Don't let these bastards get their greasy hands on you.* But I resisted the impulse. "You're worried that it'll hurt your career?"

"Well, yeah," he said, as if this was almost too obvious to mention.

I sat next to him on the couch. "I understand your concerns. But let's think about this logically. What's the worst that can happen? You'll get fined by the NBA for inappropriate behavior. Your teammates will make a few jokes. Maybe a sports journalist or two will make some disparaging remarks until somebody reminds them of Marv Albert. You're telling me that a little public embarrassment isn't worth the greater good?"

"What greater good?"

"The fans, my man. I'm talking about the fans. They love you. And not just because you're a great player. They love you because your life is more exciting and dangerous than theirs could ever be."

"You think?" He leaned forward to listen.

"They're living vicariously through you. Every time you do something outrageous, they eat it up. And that's because they wish they could be like that. They want to believe that it's not just an act, that you really are that crazy and rebellious."

"I guess."

"And you know what? When this porn comes out, there may be a few people who think it's in bad taste. But I guarantee you, your real fans will think you're a god."

"I don't know," he said, shaking his big head.

"Yes, my friend, I'm telling you: You'll be a god. It'll just confirm everything they wanted to believe about you. You know what they think, don't you? They think that after every game, you're out partying, whooping it up with beautiful women, getting laid eighteen times a night. And now they'll have *proof*."

"Yeah, but—"

"No one will ever doubt your reputation again. Every time

you walk out on the court, they'll know that you're hardcore. The other guys may talk tough, but you walked the walk. You'll make Dennis Rodman look like a goddamn Mormon."

I got off the couch, walked over to the desk and pushed away a pile of papers, letting them fall to the ground. I pulled the contract out of my back pocket and laid it on the desk.

"Just sign," I said. I was startled by my own voice. I sounded so fiercely insistent, so unwilling to be denied. J.D. must have sensed it too, because he quickly jumped off the couch and joined me next to the desk. He looked at the contract, studying it uncertainly.

"I can get out of this, right?" he asked with worried eyes. "This isn't legally binding or anything?"

"Of course not," I said, lying through my teeth. "It just says that you're considering a role in one of our films, and that you'll be available to discuss it at a later date. We're not asking for a commitment."

He wrung his hands anxiously, trying to skim the dense and confusing contract. As I watched him, he seemed so helpless. I almost felt sorry for him. He was going to sign, I was sure of it. He wasn't any more confident that he making the right decision, but I had somehow managed to intimidate him. And now he was about to make the biggest mistake of his life.

I couldn't let him go through with this. As much as I wanted to, as much as I knew I would be throwing away what might be my only chance to become rich and successful, I couldn't do it. It wasn't because I wanted to protect this idiot. If he was stupid enough to let some nobody writer talk him into throwing his career away, he probably deserved it. But if he signed that contract, and he did it because I had convinced him, then I would be no better than Ray or Clark.

For as long as I'd been working in porn, I could claim that I was an outsider. True, I didn't always like it. Occasionally I would complain that I was treated differently, that I was never made to feel like I belonged. But deep down, I was happy that they never accepted me. I wanted to keep a safe distance from their world, make it perfectly clear that I was not one of them. And as long as they called the shots, I could still cling to that belief. After all, I wasn't playing an active role in any of this. They had come to *me*. They had sought *me* out.

But this would be different. This opportunity hadn't just fallen into my lap. I had made it happen. I was responsible. And that signified something. It would have consequences. I couldn't pretend that I was just flirting with the dark side anymore. I had jumped in, head first. It might as well be my signature on that contract. I knew what I had to do.

I picked up a pen, leaned closer to J.D. "Let me show you where to sign," I said.

When our faces were just inches from each other, I began to whisper, trying not to move my lips. "Listen to me," I said. "I can get you out of this."

"What?"

"Be quiet." I motioned towards the window behind us, but just slightly, careful not to be too obvious. "They're watching us."

Without moving his head, his eyes shifted to the window and then back to me. "Just follow my lead," I whispered.

I handed him the pen but he knew enough not to take it. "What do you mean you won't sign?" I yelled, loud enough so that Ray and Clark would hear every word.

"I...," J.D. looked at me helplessly, unsure how to respond. I tried to give him subtle cues with my face, silently prompting him. "I won't sign," he said, but not with the confidence we needed to sell it.

"Don't be a fool," I hissed. "This is a huge opportunity for you."

"Uh, I—"

"I can do *what*? Stick this contract up my ass?"

"Yeah." He was still too tentative, but at least he was playing along.

"You fucking cocksucker," I roared, baring my teeth. "Nobody talks to me like that. I should have you fucking killed."

That last bit was for Ray. I knew he'd like that line. But it made me nervous all the same. I was not in the habit of threatening large muscular black men who had a good three feet on me.

I advanced on J.D., pushing him towards door while trying to make it appear that I was actually following him, attempting to cut him off. It involved some complicated choreography, and it didn't help that J.D. was totally confused, thus forcing me to do all the work.

"Where the hell do you think you're going?" I screamed.

J.D. almost tripped over backwards a few times, which would have ruined everything, but he eventually got his bearings back. He began to move on his own power, and even flailed his arms a few times, like we were actually involved in a game of keep-away. A nice touch, I thought. He reached for the door, but I placed an arm in front of him, blocking his exit.

"You can't leave. We're not done here!"

He pushed my arm away, but I came right back, throwing my body across the door.

"I'm serious. You walk out on us and you'll regret it."

With his huge hands, he grabbed me by the shoulders and

picked me up. It was all too easy for him. He held me there for a moment, dangling in the air like a rag doll. When it had been made abundantly clear that I was no physical match for him, he gently dropped me to the floor, a few feet to the left of the door.

Before he marched out, he looked towards the window, speaking directly to it. "Thanks anyway, guys," he said loudly. "No hard feelings."

He turned back to me and his face was filled with so much anger, I actually thought he might hurt me. "And you," he snarled, "you're a fucking asshole."

He opened the door and began to walk out. But at the last second, he smiled so quickly that I almost didn't notice it. "Thanks," he whispered.

"Fuck you!" I screamed, but the door had already slammed shut behind him.

I stormed around the office, knocking things over and kicking the wall. I wanted them to think I was furious, so disappointed that I couldn't control my temper tantrum. But inside, I was laughing. I had actually pulled it off.

As I continued making a mess of their office, I heard the faint echo of someone screaming from behind the one-way mirror. I couldn't be sure, but it almost sounded like Ray and Clark were tackling each other again.

Good, I thought. Throw a few punches for me.

I was having nightmares again. Strange, unsettling nightmares that made me afraid to go to sleep. In one of them, I'm a grizzly old pornographer testifying before a grand jury, possibly the Meese Commission. For some reason, I'm in a wheelchair. I'm not sure if I'm paralyzed or just too lazy to walk on my own.

I'm surrounded by a gaggle of porn actresses, all of whom are dressed in flimsy nightgowns. They're giggling, tickling me, wiping the drool from my chin with a satin cloth. My skin is oily and covered in rashes, but there's a smugness in my face. I take a sick pride in what I do for a living. I preach to the commissioners about First Amendment rights, the value of free speech. "Our founding fathers wanted this," I say. "It was their dream that one day, all men, regardless of race or creed, would be able to enjoy movies about anal sex."

Most nights, the nightmares would cause me to wake up screaming. But tonight, the day after my encounter with the NBA player, I sat up in bed with a newfound sense of clarity. I nudged my wife until she opened her eyes.

"What's wrong?" she asked, blearily.

"I want to leave L.A."

She sighed. "And go where? Back to Chicago?"

"No. I don't know. Maybe. There's no porn there. Or if there is, I don't know anybody involved."

She tried to change my mind. We weren't just living in L.A. for the porn, she said. What about my screenplay? As far as we knew, my agent was still pitching it to studios. It could break for me any day. And what of her aspirations to write for television? She was getting so close. If we could just be patient, wait just a little longer.

Perhaps, I said. But I reminded her that it had been over a year since we moved to L.A., and nothing had changed. Agents called now and again, occasionally rewarding us with a free meal. But the studio meetings they promised never took place. The checks they all but guaranteed us never arrived in the mail. We were no closer to a legitimate writing deal today than when we first arrived in this foul city.

"So you just want to quit?" she said.

"It's not quitting," I said. "It's running away."

"Is that any better?"

"Yes, it's better. Quitting is about weakness. We're not weak. We're afraid."

"Afraid of what?"

"Of everything. Of the porn industry. Of our agents. Of everything this city represents. I don't know about you, but I can't take it anymore. I'm tired of wanting so desperately for the right people to notice me, and then being terrified that they'll notice me at the wrong moment. I'm tired of constantly worrying about my future. I'm tired of writing what they want me to write, being who they want me to be just because I think they might pay for it. I'm tired of looking over my shoulder, waiting for them to find me out, expose me as a fraud. I'm tired of knowing that it could all end, that everything I ever wanted to do with my life could be taken away. And I'm tired of wondering how my dreams ever became so small that anybody could take them away so easily."

I took my wife's hand, squeezed it. "There's no shame in leaving," I said. "Because we're leaving of our own free will. We're not losers, we're *cowards*."

My wife started to speak, but stopped herself. I could see the resignation in her face. She wanted to tell me I was wrong, wanted to convince me that L.A. wasn't a lost cause, or at least convince herself. But she didn't have the energy for it anymore. I like to think that a part of her knew I was right.

"Okay," she said. "I'll start packing tomorrow."

10

"Can we get a few more girls on that trampoline?"

Ray was speaking to Clark, but for some reason I felt inclined to answer. "I don't think that's such a good idea," I said. "It's already a little crowded as it is."

I'm not sure what compelled me to contradict Ray in front of his entire cast and crew. Maybe it was the knowledge that I would soon be away from this place and I had nothing left to lose. Maybe it was the warm Malibu sun and lack of smog which had a surprisingly positive effect on my mood. Or maybe I just liked the idea of pissing Ray off.

Ray turned to me with a blank stare, as if he wasn't quite sure who I was or what I was doing here. He'd been successfully ignoring me all morning which I assumed was his way of punishing me. He was still furious that I'd allowed the NBA player to get away. As far as he was concerned, I could no longer be trusted. And I was fine with that. He could give me the cold shoulder all he wanted. It was better than the alternative. It'd been weeks since he'd last threatened to have me killed which, for Ray, was a personal record.

"I'd have to agree," Clark said, sensing the tension. "It's getting pretty tight up there. We don't want them to start tripping over each other and breaking their necks."

Ray snorted contemptuously. "The fuck I care," he mumbled.

"I just think we should be a little more careful. The most important thing is to make sure that nobody gets hurt."

"No," Ray snapped. "The most fucking important thing is to create the right visual effect. This is the most pivotal scene in the movie, and it needs to be a full-on spectacle. I'm talking about sensory overload, jiggling flesh flying from every direction, a goddamn feeding frenzy of erotic imagery. But I can't do that if you don't get off my fucking back and let me do my fucking job!"

Ray had no reason to be concerned. If it was a spectacle he wanted, he couldn't have asked for much more. The set was filled with women, nearly fifty in all, most of them naked or in some state of undress. They were jumping on trampolines, throwing judo punches at each other, levitating in the air while attached to bungee cords. It was like an obscene side-show carnival. There was so much activity taking place, my eyes didn't know where to focus.

When I'd written this particular scene, I imagined a surreal training camp for James Bond girls. At the time, it had seemed like a hilarious concept. But I never thought it would end up being so disturbing. There were just too many bodies in motion, their small frames being twisted and pulled in directions that God (and certainly not their plastic surgeons) had ever intended. It was far too much information on the inner workings of the human body. Their skin was literally being stretched to the breaking point, exposing their ribcages (and in some cases, implants) in graphic detail.

Of course, it didn't help matters that the entire shoot was taking place outside. We were at a private mansion in the Malibu mountains which had been "loaned" to Ray by an old friend who owed him a favor. We weren't allowed to enter the main living area but were given full access to a huge back yard that went on for miles and afforded a spectacular view of the ocean. It seemed like the ideal setting for a porno, and very well might have been, except that the lack of shade was wreaking havoc on the actresses.

The sun acted as a cruel microscope, exposing every imperfection that might have gone unnoticed under less harsh lighting conditions. The makeup people rushed onto the set every few minutes, slinging powder like haywire crop-dusters but it was a losing battle. After a full morning of sun exposure and extreme physical exercise, the women resembled skeletons covered in a thin layer of latex.

Ignoring Clark, Ray instructed another actress to climb onto the main trampoline, and filming resumed. Clark sighed and muttered something to one of the crew members. They rifled through a small box marked "First Aid," and Clark's face went pale. He walked back towards me and collapsed onto a lounge chair.

"This is not going to end well," he muttered to himself.

Needless to say, my wife and I had not left L.A. yet. It wasn't that we'd changed our minds. Far from it. Our bags were packed, everything we owned was in boxes. It was just a matter of when to leave. And, of course, where we would go. Chicago seemed like the best option but it just felt too much like a step backwards. We weren't sure if we could face our old friends, explain to them how L.A. had beaten us. Best to go someplace where nobody knew us, where we could have a fresh start. New York, maybe? It seemed promising but how could we possibly afford it? We'd need real jobs and, after our year in L.A., we had no marketable skills other than a proficiency at trivia and writing porn.

Even if we decided to take the chance and head east, getting there would take money. Money that we didn't have. Renting a truck to haul our belongings across the country wouldn't be cheap and at this point, we were down to our last pennies. If we didn't get some hard cash soon, we could be stuck in L.A. indefinitely.

As luck would have it, it was around this time that I got a call from Clark. After countless rewrites, the script I'd written for him was finally going into production. And I was invited to witness the proceedings. I wanted to say no. I really did. After my last experience on a porn set, I was none too eager to repeat the ordeal. But I didn't have much of a choice. If I failed to make an appearance, there was a fairly good chance that I wouldn't be paid.

As I'd learned, nobody involved in a porno is compensated for their services until the day of production. I suppose that I could have asked Clark to mail me a check. But where would he send it? Even if I did have an address to give him, did I really want him to know how to find me? It was a moot point anyway. We needed the money now. I would just have to show up and claim what was owed to me.

But that was only part of my reason for showing up. I also wanted to let Ray and Clark know that I was leaving. It didn't seem wise to just disappear without telling anybody. They would notice my absence, and might even become concerned. They would look for me, I felt certain. And I didn't want that. I would just have to come right out and be honest with them. Well, maybe not *completely* honest. That could get ugly. I'd skirt around the truth a little, pick only the facts that they needed to know. Or better yet, I'd tell them a flat-out lie. Yes, that would do just fine. And it'd be less likely to result in a screaming match. I'd just come up with some compelling reason for why I had to leave California immediately. It had to sound believable, something within the realm of possibility. And it couldn't be anything that they might check up on. My alibi must be airtight.

So I went to the set with a newfound sense of purpose. I was not just another peeping Tom. I was after something more significant than leering voyeurism. This was about money and closure. Nothing more than that.

Nope.

Seriously.

"Clark, please, I don't want to do this."

"Relax. It'll just take a minute. You need to lighten up. This is supposed to be fun."

Clark pushed down on my shoulders, forcing me to sit on the stool. He backed away and signaled for the two women standing behind him to join me. They were actresses, the female "stars" of our film, and they both looked as enthusiastic about participating in this impromptu photo session as I was. They slowly positioned themselves on my lap, touching only as much of me as was absolutely necessary. I could feel their bony asses digging into me, and I had to shift my legs to keep from collapsing under their combined body weight. We exchanged strained smiles and I tried to appear indifferent, as if I was perfectly accustomed to being cuddled by strange naked women.

Clark studied us for a moment, arranging our limbs like department store mannequins. He placed their arms across my shoulders, urging them to lean into me, until their breasts were mere inches away from my face. A nipple jabbed me in the eye, temporarily blinding me.

"There," he said, finally satisfied. "That's perfect."

I'm not sure how it had come to this. I was supposed to be far away from here by now, driving back towards civilization with a check in my pocket and the sweet relief that I would never have to see these people again. But somehow it hadn't worked out that way. I had been tricked.

From the moment I arrived, Clark had been avoiding me. He must have suspected my intentions because he managed to evade me at every turn, always finding some excuse to make a hasty retreat. At first, I didn't mind being ignored. I'd never ventured into the hills of Malibu before and I was shocked at just how beautiful they were. The sun was somehow warmer here, the smog less imposing. And the mansion, as promised, was like some castle in the sky. I'd never seen anything so luxurious in my entire life. It wouldn't be right to take off in such a hurry.

The first few hours passed quickly. I watched them shoot the "trampoline" montage, which they somehow completed without any major injuries. And then, much to my delight, they moved on to scenes that involved actual speaking roles. And it wasn't quite so awful as I'd expected. Oh sure, it was bad. The actors stumbled over their lines and occasionally attempted accents that were totally unnecessary. The story, which had been trimmed to only the bare essentials, was even less coherent than I remembered. There were too many characters and none of what they said or did made any sense whatsoever. The plot, if there actually was one anymore, was about everything and nothing, managing to be both convoluted and one-dimensional at exactly the same time. I had no idea what was happening at any given moment and I *wrote* it.

But it still worked, primarily because the script was filled with just the right amount of visual distractions. I had consciously included as many outlandish costume changes and absurd theatrics as humanly possible, hoping that if the action was fast-paced and silly enough, it would somehow compensate for the lack of any comprehensible narrative.

After a full morning, we broke for lunch and I was finally able to corner Clark. I told him that I was leaving L.A., and I think I said something about New York. I don't know why I felt the need to share that particular piece of information. It just came out of my mouth before I could stop myself. Though I immediately regretted it, I was relieved that I'd been brave enough to say anything at all.

He'd nodded through my entire explanation, as if he understood completely. But when I finished, he'd dragged me to a private corner of the set, insisting that I pose for an intimate candid with the leading ladies. It would be a souvenir, he said. A memento to remember my day at the porn set. But I knew exactly what was going on. This was not a friendly gesture. This was bribery. He was trying to tempt me with sex, surround me with beautiful women so that I'd see the error in my decision.

I was in no mood for any of this. It didn't help matters that I was coming down with the flu. I'd woken up that morning feeling slightly queasy and I assumed it was just nerves. But over the course of the day, my symptoms had become increasingly alarming. I'd developed a high fever and my muscles were so stiff that I couldn't move without intense discomfort. I was shivering, sweating so profusely that my armpits had been stained yellow. I just wanted to go home and pass out, crawl into bed for a few days and sleep this thing off. The last thing I needed was to have my personal space invaded by a pair of floozies who, for all I knew, were walking petri dishes for any number of infectious viruses.

The photographer was taking his time, pausing every so often to check his light meter or take another swig from a bottle of light beer. Something wet and warm was dribbling down my upper lip but I was powerless to stop it. My arms were pinned under naked flesh and I wouldn't be able to break free without drawing attention to my leaking nose. I could feel a sneeze coming on and struggled to choke it back but that had the same effect as throwing a blanket over dynamite. My throat erupted in a phlegmy gurgling, emitting an odor that smelled not unlike rotten asparagus. The women glared at me but I pretended not to notice.

I saw a strange man appear behind Clark. He was grotesquely obese and bore more than a passing resemblance to Marlon Brando circa *Island of Dr. Moreau*. His thinning gray hair had been slicked back into a greasy comb-over and his Hawaiian shirt was unbuttoned to the waist, allowing his impressive man-nipples to peek out like two hamsters.

The fat man tugged at Clark's sleeve and they greeted each other with fierce back-slapping. The fat man whispered something into Clark's ear, glancing at the women with hungry eyes. Clark nodded and instructed the photographer to take a break. He led the fat man towards us and introduced him as the company's lawyer. The women sighed miserably, well aware of what was coming next.

"You want a picture with the girls?" Clark asked. The fat man shook his head eagerly, and Clark turned to me. "Eric, would you mind?"

He didn't have to ask me twice. I jumped up so quickly that I nearly knocked both women to the ground. I retreated behind the photographer and watched as the fat lawyer carefully lowered himself onto the stool. He summoned the women to join him, slapping his chubby knees like a degenerate Santa Claus.

"Listen, Clark, I really need to be going now," I said.

I don't think Clark even heard me. He was too busy yelling directions at the women, telling them to arch their backs, pout their lips, anything that might distract from their repulsed expressions. The fat lawyer couldn't have cared less that they found him so objectionable. He smiled vulgarly for the camera, his ruddy face framed by naked breasts.

I couldn't leave without my check, and Clark knew it. He was trying to stall for as long as possible, breaking down my spirit until I'd agree to anything. But given the condition of my immune system, I couldn't last much longer. It took everything I had just to remain standing upright and it was only a matter of time before my body crumbled into a gray, lifeless lump. I had to take action immediately.

"Okay then," I said. "If that's all you need from me, I'll be on my way."

I slowly stepped backwards, as if I fully intended to slink away whether acknowledged by Clark or not. It was a blatant attempt to call his bluff and Clark was having none of it. He continued to ignore me, maintaining an excellent poker face, but I was sure he was watching me out of the corner of his eye, considering his options.

"It was nice working with you," I said, holding up my hand

in a farewell wave. "Good luck with everything. I'll just be—"

I'd managed only to get a few feet between us before Clark spun around and grabbed my arm. "Why are you doing this?" he asked, his voice tinged with real panic. "Is it me? Is it something I've done?"

"No, no, not at all," I reassured him. "You've been great."

"So, it's Raymond? Did he threaten you again? I told him to stop doing that."

"No, it's—"

"I know he can be a little gruff but you can't take him so seriously. He's just a big puppy dog once you get to know him."

"This has nothing to do with either of you. It's just time for me to move on."

Clark's face contorted into a pained grimace. "I had no idea you were so unhappy. Why didn't you come to me sooner? I could have tried to help. I could have made it better. But you never gave me a chance."

"It's not like that."

"I thought we had a connection, you and I. I thought we understood each other."

"We do. I mean—"

"You've been like a son to me. And this is how you treat me?"

He was clutching me so tightly that I could feel his fingernails digging into my skin. I'd expected him to be upset, but I never imagined he would get so hysterical. Surely this wasn't the first time that he'd lost an employee. People left the porn industry every day, on an almost hourly basis, so he must have seen this coming.

"You're taking this too personally," I said.

"How can I not take it personally? You're telling me that

you want me out of your life, that you never want to see me again. Did you really think that wouldn't hurt me?"

"Well, I don't—"

"I know you're ashamed of me. I know that you hate what I do for a living. But to completely shut me out like this, it's just not fair."

"I—"

"Do you have any idea what this is like for me?" Clark pleaded. "Do you know how it feels to lose everybody that you ever cared about? *Do you*?"

He was talking to me but he seemed to be looking right through me. It was as if he were having a conversation with somebody else, somebody that only he could see. At that moment, I realized that I was dealing with a man with deep psychological problems more complex than I could fathom. The calm demeanor that had made him seem so much more rational and healthy than anybody else in this business was just a thin façade, masking a raging psychosis that had just been waiting for the right moment to come bubbling to the surface. By sheer coincidence, my leaving had triggered some painful memory that he'd suppressed for God knows how long. And now I was directly in the middle of a full-on psychosomatic backlash, thrust into the role of stand-in for whatever bizarre family issues had been haunting him.

"Please don't give up on me," he said. "I can be a better man. I can make you proud of me. But you have to give me another chance."

"Okay," I said. It was a dangerous game to be playing but I didn't see as I had much choice. Far be it from me to refuse an emotionally vulnerable pornographer.

He embraced me, gently stroking my head as he pinned it

against his chest. "I love you," he blubbered. "I really do. I really, really do."

"Thanks, I..."

We were interrupted by the piercing sounds of high-pitched squealing, and turned to see both women frantically brushing at their chests. While Clark wasn't looking, the lawyer had gotten a bit too frisky and attempted to nuzzle their cleavage. They'd pushed him away but not before he'd left an oily stain on each of their breasts.

"What is it?" one of the women screamed. "Get it off me! Get it off!"

It was quite remarkable, actually. The stain was an almost perfect impression of the lawyer's face, reminiscent of the Shroud of Turin. The photographer threw a towel at the women and they scrubbed it against their skin to little effect. They only managed to smear it, covering their breasts in the tar-like substance.

"It's not coming off! Fucking hell, it's not coming off!!"

Clark released me and rubbed a finger across his eyes, wiping away a tear. In a matter of seconds, he was back in control, instantly morphing back into the role of producer. It was as if his mental meltdown had been a brief indiscretion, as easily cast aside and forgotten as an old shirt.

"Okay, ladies, settle down," he said, smiling calmly. "I'll get the hose."

After the women had been scoured and polished until they were squeaky clean, Clark disappeared yet again. I don't know how he did it. One minute he was standing right in front of me and the next, he was gone. I had to admire his tenacity. I had never met someone so skilled at avoiding confrontation.

I had little choice but to loiter around the set and wait. I suppose I could have asked Ray for my check but he was looking unusually tense, what with the pressures of trying to squeeze an entire week's worth of shooting into one afternoon. Combined with the fact that he was already angry with me, interrupting him with requests for money seemed like a sure-fire recipe for disaster. No, it was best just to lay low awhile and let Clark tire himself out. He was bound to get bored with this cat-and-mouse routine eventually.

The next couple of hours were mostly a blur. I was so deranged with fever that I regularly drifted in and out of consciousness. I can only recall a few hazy memories that may or may not have actually taken place.

I remember at one point noticing a golf cart perched on a cliff overlooking the set. It was too far away to be certain, but there appeared to be an extremely old man sitting behind the wheel. I watched him for some time, wondering who he was and what he was doing up there, not to mention how he could have possibly gotten a golf cart up into these mountains. He was eerily still, his body remaining perfectly motionless. It occurred to me that he might be dead. He could very well be a corpse, the decaying remains of some poor fool who'd roamed too far from home and gotten hopelessly lost.

I pointed out the old man to a crewmember, who informed me that he was "The Money." I was advised not to make direct eye contact with him and never, under any circumstances, block his view of the sex. "Just forget about him," I was told. "After awhile, you won't even know he's there."

I also began to appreciate why more pornos aren't filmed outside. A number of scenes were cut short by the sudden appearance of low-flying planes. The first time might have been a coincidence. But then the plane reappeared again and shortly thereafter returned for a third fly-by. Soon other planes were cruising overhead, flying so close to the ground that some of the actresses were being knocked over by strong gusts of wind. Each time it happened, Ray stopped the cameras and had the women hide under towels. But when the planes kept coming back, Ray became enraged and began throwing lawn chairs and screaming obscenities.

"Rue the day," he howled, his face going so red that the veins in his neck threatened to burst. "Rue the fucking day!!"

Far from intimidating them, Ray only managed to rile up the pilots and they began playing chicken with him. They aimed their planes towards the ground, chasing him down the length of the yard. Ray waited until they'd left, and then, against all logic, came running back into the yard, screaming at the planes until they returned and chased him yet again. The crew thought it was hilarious, if only because of the obvious illusions to *North By Northwest*. But Ray wouldn't quit. He just kept coming back for more, repeating the cycle of taunting and chasing, as if he thought next time would be different. It was humiliating to watch him, unaware that he was making a complete ass of himself, running across the lawn like some confused dog.

Eventually I wandered off the set, looking for somewhere to escape all the chaos and maybe lie down for awhile. The flu had really started to hit hard and I was beginning to worry that I might be trapped here forever. I'd long since forgotten where I'd parked my car, and even if I managed to find it again, I didn't have the strength to drive myself home. Only my wife knew where I was and she wouldn't know how to locate me. I could be stuck here for days before the helicopters finally spotted be and by then it could be too late.

I ended up seeking refuge at a gazebo, if only because it was the only spot within a three-mile radius not already overcrowded with naked people. I collapsed onto a bench and curled into the fetal position. It was hardly comfortable but I was too exhausted to care. I just needed a short nap, long enough to start feeling like a human again.

I'm not sure how long I was passed out there. When I finally opened my eyes again, there was a woman looking down at me. She had long, flowing black hair and her face was illuminated by warm light, giving her an almost saintly appearance. I just naturally assumed that I was dead. I was in heaven and this was an angel, coming to take me to the Other Side. 'Shit,' I thought. 'I had to go and die at a porn set. I hope that doesn't go on my permanent record.'

The woman placed a hand on my forehead and frowned. "My God, you're burning up."

She sat next to me on the bench, and I realized that she wasn't an angel at all. It was Ginger. Ginger with the elastic limbs. Ginger who hated writers, particularly writers who tried to pass themselves off as porn actors named Felipe. Though I wasn't happy to see her, I was thankful that she'd at least bothered to put on some clothes. She was wearing a bathrobe and sneakers, and for some reason she was carrying around a backpack which I could only assume was used to store her beauty aids, script and... what did they call it? Sexual accessories.

I tried to speak but was cut off by another violent coughing fit. She studied me with a concerned expression, and then reached into her backpack and pulled out a book. I recognized it instantly. It was the *Merck Manual of Diagnosis and Therapy*, seventeenth edition. Twenty-five thousand pages of pure medical terror, listing symptoms of every disease known to man. I owned a copy as well but kept mine next to the bed for late night anxiety attacks. I'd never met anybody who carried the *Merck* around with them. The thing probably weighed more than she did.

I noticed that she'd outlined certain passages with a yellow highlighter and she'd scribbled extensive notes in the margins. This wasn't the work of a casual hypochondriac. She was a *professional*. If I wasn't careful, she's have me running towards the nearest emergency room, whimpering about diseases I couldn't even pronounce.

"A cough and fever," she said, skimming through the book. "What other symptoms do you have?"

"A headache," I stammered.

"Hmmm. That could be a lot of things. You could have a stroke, a spine disorder, a brain abscess, acute intracranial infection, severe hypertension, cerebral hypoxia, and any number of diseases of the eyes, nose, throat, teeth, ears and cervical vertebrae. I don't want to scare you but there's also a chance you could have cancer."

She must have seen the terror in my face because she began stroking my hand, smiling with a gentle affection. "Don't worry, you're probably fine. I just mentioned cancer because I'm obsessed with it."

"Is that right?"

"It's kinda a hobby of mine. I've read every cancer textbook, every newspaper clipping, anything I can get my hands on. I've done volunteer work at Cedars-Sinai just so I could observe the cancer patients."

"No kidding?"

"My mom thinks I'm paranoid but the way I see it, I'm just preparing myself for the inevitable."

I'd become so accustomed to her hostility, it was odd to

have her speaking like this, sharing secrets about her private life that I'm sure most of her fellow actors knew almost nothing about. I don't think she intended to forge a friendship, it had just happened by accident. Simply by being sick and allowing her to diagnose me, I'd somehow given her reason to trust me.

She rifled through her backpack again and removed a plastic baggie filled with small yellow pills. "Here," she said, handing me one of the pills. "Take this."

"What is it?"

"I'm not sure but I got it from a doctor friend of mine. It'll freeze out the pain receptors in your central nervous system. It won't cure you but it'll numb you up for awhile."

I rolled the tiny pill across my palm, considering what to do. It didn't seem wise to accept drugs from a woman I hardly knew — particularly when the drugs had come from an unmarked plastic baggie. This seemed to fall under the "don't take candy from strangers" line of reasoning that I'd been warned about since childhood. But, on the other hand, I felt terrible. If these mystery pills could provide even a moment's relief, surely it was worth the risk.

"It's perfectly safe," she said. "You want to feel better or what?"

There were at least a thousand rational reasons not to do this but I was long past thinking rationally. I threw the pill into my mouth and swallowed hard. I closed my eyes and prepared for the worst. But nothing happened. No sharp pains, no seizures, no side effects whatsoever that might reasonably result from consuming a toxic pharmaceutical.

Well, I thought, so far so good. I rested my head on the cold cement and waited for the drug to take effect. Ginger had returned to her *Merck* and seemed to be engrossed in one of her favorite chapters.

"Listen to this," she said. "'Pleural effusions, if present, should be drained if symptomatic and followed by reaccumulation. If the effusion reaccumulates rapidly, thoracostomy tube drainage and sclerosing agents should be used.'"

"What does that mean?" I asked.

She looked up, her eyes aglow with giddy excitement. "I have no idea, but isn't it *terrifying*?"

11

"It's a pussy."

Clark and I tilted our heads, trying for a better look. The hideous object on display before us only vaguely resembled female genitalia. It looked like a pumpkin that had been smashed down the center with a sledgehammer and then painted red. And though I hardly considered myself an expert on such matters, I was pretty sure that most vaginas don't come equipped with razor-sharp fangs.

The man responsible for this monstrosity was holding it in his arms, cradling it like a small child. He was dressed entirely in black, his long hair pulled back into a tight ponytail. I assumed that he was a director, if only because he looked the part.

"I spent my life savings on this thing," he said. "Had it built from my own design. Isn't it fucking beautiful?"

Although I wouldn't have used exactly those words, I had to respect the craftsmanship that'd gone into it. It seemed to be made from little more than papier-mâché and some sort of foam padding, but the finished product was shockingly gruesome. This was truly the handiwork of a mentally impaired mind, a chilling incarnation of one man's sexual demons.

"Why the teeth?" Clark asked.

"Because this isn't your ordinary gigantic vagina."

"Apparently not."

"It's a *man-eating* gigantic vagina."

"Oh, sure, of course."

"It fucks like a normal vagina. But when it's finished, it devours the guy in a carnivorous frenzy."

"Have you been seeing that therapist I told you about?" Clark asked.

Just moments before, I had been ready for anything. My symptoms were finally starting to subside. In fact, I felt stronger than ever. It was like a surge of electricity was coursing through my veins. My mind was alert and my body was wired with adrenaline. I'd gone looking for Clark, certain that I would be able to handle him this time.

Little did I know that I would be thwarted yet again, much less by a vagina with huge, razor-sharp incisors. You can forgive me if I never saw it coming.

"Come on," the man whined. "You're telling me you don't think this is brilliant?"

"I'm just not sure if castration anxiety is the emotion we want to instill in our audience," Clark said.

Something about the director seemed familiar. I couldn't put my finger on it but I had the distinct feeling that I'd met him somewhere before.

"Well, I think you're wrong," he said. "This is sexy stuff. It's Freudian."

"Freud is sexy?"

"Fuck yeah Freud is sexy. Fucking your mom? That's sexy. Losing your penis in a blood-thirsty vagina with violent feminist tendencies? That, my friend, is *sexy*."

Suddenly, it all came back. That long night on the set of my first porno. His bumbling performance. Our tête-à-tête out in the parking lot where I'd somehow convinced him that he should be a director. I didn't think he'd taken me seriously but apparently my pep talk had done the trick.

"Ian?" I asked, though I hadn't intended to say it out loud.

They both turned, only just now realizing that I was standing there. Ian didn't seem to recognize me but a huge smile flashed across Clark's face.

"What do you think, Eric?" he asked.

"About what?"

He pointed towards the vagina. "Is there a film here? Could we make this work?"

"Well, I guess. I mean, it's... interesting."

"So you'd be willing to write the script?"

"Me? Oh, no, I didn't... I don't... No, not really."

Clark frowned, as if my refusal to offer my services had been a deal-breaker. "That's a shame," he said. I knew exactly what he was doing. He'd made me the fall guy, letting me take all the blame for turning down Ian. It was an inspired tactical move and I had walked right into it.

"It's a great idea, don't get me wrong," I said. "But I'm just not sure if I'm the right person for the job."

"Why the hell not?" Ian demanded.

"I'm a comedy writer. I write jokes. You're tackling issues that are far too complex. I mean, you've clearly put a lot of thought into this and you've got something here that could very well have major cultural and artistic implications. I couldn't even begin to grasp the socio-sexual politics of it."

"The *what*?"

I couldn't believe what I was saying. I didn't owe him an explanation. And I certainly didn't need to indulge his ego with a lot of pseudo-intellectual gibberish. But I didn't have the heart to be honest and admit that I had no interest whatsoever in writing anything having to do with a man-eating vagina.

"It's not complex at all," Ian objected. "You're telling me you've never been afraid of a vagina?"

"No."

"You've never looked at a chick's puss and wondered if it might kill you?" he insisted. "Never even considered the possibility that it might be able to suck out your soul?"

"Not really, no."

Ian looked at me with disbelief, like I had just admitted to something inconceivable. "Why are you in porn?" he asked.

I was about to answer him when I heard the growling. It sounded like the low, rumbling snarl of a dog before it attacked. I told myself that it was just my imagination. It couldn't be what I thought it was. It just wasn't possible. I slowly turned my head, just enough to catch a quick peek.

The goddamn vagina was breathing.

"Sweet Jesus!" I screamed.

I backed away so quickly that I tripped over my own legs, falling to the ground. Clark and Ian looked at me like they hadn't the slightest idea what I was carrying on about.

"Get it away from me!" I howled. "Get it away!"

"I think somebody's had too much sun," Ian remarked, not once noticing that the vagina he was holding had somehow come to life.

Clark knelt next to me, calmly assessing my mental state. "It's okay, buddy," he said, in his best soothing voice. "You're fine. Everything's fine. Nobody wants to hurt you."

"Fucking hell," I whimpered. "What is it? How did it—?"

"I want to help you," Clark said. "But you have to tell me what's wrong."

Couldn't he see it? Couldn't he hear the growling? I pointed towards the vagina which was trying to squirm out of Ian's arms. It barked at me, snapping its powerful jaws like it wanted to rip into my flesh. But Clark didn't even flinch. He was completely oblivious to the fact that we were about to be savagely gored by a beast made of papier-mâché.

I shielded my face with both hands. I couldn't watch any more. It was too horrible.

"I need you to relax," Clark said. "I don't know what's happening here but I'll take care of it. You can trust me."

I let him pull my hands away which, as it turned out, was a huge mistake. Clark's skin had taken on a dark reddish hue and was now covered in thick, reptilian scales. Two tiny horns were affixed to his forehead and he had somehow grown a tail which lazily curled across his shoulders, occasionally swatting at the air. His eyes were empty sockets and wisps of fire trickled from his mouth when he spoke.

"Trust me," he hissed, flicking his forked tongue. "Truuuust me."

Ian was struggling to contain the vagina which had almost managed to break free. "Bad girl," he snapped. "Don't make me get the leash." He was naked and his shriveled penis flapped against his stomach like a boiled shrimp. He also had breasts. Huge, veiny breasts that looked diseased, as if they'd been constructed from long dead tissue.

Well, I thought, this can't be right.

I made a run for it. I didn't know where I was going but I had to get out of there, get away from these freaks. As I sprinted through the backyard, I saw hundreds of porn actors, all of them naked, all of them horribly deformed in some way. Limbs were missing, heads were enlarged to an obscene size, hair was growing in places where it shouldn't. A few of them were midgets.

"You can't escape," one of the actors called to me. "You're one of us now."

"The fuck I am," I screamed back.

Their numbers were growing and they soon had me surrounded. At every turn, there were more of them, blocking my path, reaching out to me with white, misshapen arms.

"We accept you!" they chanted in a dull monotone. "We accept you! One of us! One of us!"

I shoved my way through the bodies and leapt over a hedge, unaware that there was nothing on the other side. I fell hard, tumbling through crabgrass, dirt flying everywhere. The actors gathered on the cliff's edge, watching me plummet to an almost certain death. And still they kept chanting.

"Gooble gobble! Gooble gobble! One of us! One of us!"

It hurt a little at first, but when I stopped fighting and let my body go limp, it was like being carried away by the mountain winds. It wasn't the best way to travel but I was making great time. At this rate, I would be home before sundown.

Vibrant colors swirled around me, pulling me into a vortex of beautiful light. I knew that I was still falling but I wasn't afraid. I was being guided. I was being led to safety. The voices were growing more distant, their morbid chanting gradually fading

"We accept you. We accept you."

until there was nothing left

"One of us. One of us."

but a whisper

"We acce—"

and then

they were

gone.

FADE IN:

EXT. DESERT - DAY

Somewhere in the middle of a bleak and desolate wasteland. The vast, rolling hills of white sand seem to go on forever. The sun beats down hard, scorching the earth. No living thing could survive out here for very long.

I lurch forward with my last ounce of strength. My clothes are dirty and torn, and I'm delirious from the unrelenting heat and lack of hydration. I begin to wobble, my legs no longer able to offer much support and I collapse onto the dusty terrain. I lay there for a moment wondering if I can go on. It's useless. The most I can hope for now is that death will come quickly.

Bathed in brilliant light, I lift my head, squinting into the glare. Though my vision is blurred, something is emerging from the desert vapors: the faint silhouette of a man walking towards me. He's dressed in a buckskin outfit. His skin is too white, almost translucent.

In the blink of an eye, he is standing right in front of me. I recognize something in his face. The pale skin tone, the five o'clock shadow, the sunken cheekbones. Why, of course, it's Jerry Stahl.

JERRY STAHL

Gotten a little lost? You're just going to wander through the desert until you find your way home?

ME

Doesn't look like I have much choice. Unless you'd be kind enough to point me towards the nearest major highway.

STAHL

(*shakes head.*)

You know what your problem is? You're a cultural elitist. You think you're so much better than the rest of us — that you're the only one with any creative integrity. You've had this smug sense of superiority ever since you moved to L.A. What do you want anyway? Does the entire city need to make a public apology for not living up to your expectations?

ME

That would be a start.

STAHL

I don't know why you're so surprised. You obviously wanted to feel this way. And it couldn't have worked out more perfectly. I mean, did you actually think that writing porn *wouldn't* disappoint you?

ME

I just thought—

STAHL

You thought you could change it, but that's bullshit. You never believed for a second that you would be able to make a difference, did you? You only got into porn because you knew it would confirm your worst fears about Hollywood. You wanted to be a part of something where failure was inevitable. This way, you wouldn't have to waste your time striving for something better only to be let down. It was a shortcut to disillusionment, a preemptive strike on creative insignificance.

ME

No, that's not right at all.

STAHL

Because you were meant for better things. You've got too much credibility to waste your talents writing hack scripts. They'll never be able to appreciate your capacity for greatness.

ME

There's no need for the sarcasm.

STAHL

If you're so original, then how do you explain this contrived story line? The constant dream sequences, the lame homage to *Freaks*.

ME

Yeah, but—

STAHL

And now this. You're in the desert, high on hallucinogenics, having visions. You're telling me this isn't just a little derivative? It's a film cliché, not to mention a direct rip-off of Oliver Stone. If you're such a creative genius, how come you couldn't come up with a better plot device?

ME

Well, I don't—

STAHL

And you couldn't even settle for a real shaman. It just *had* to be a celebrity. How could you possibly experience a true moment of spiritual enlightenment without being visited by a famous guest star? And why the sudden conversion to screenplay format? Is this supposed to be symbolic of something, or have you just gotten lazy?

ME

I-I don't know.

STAHL

You're a product of Hollywood, same as us. It was in your blood long before you moved here. You can run away but it's not going to change anything.

ME

Now, hold on. You're not being fair. I'd agree that the whole desert hallucination conceit is a bit hackneyed, but casting you as my spirit guide clearly wasn't a random choice.

STAHL

Is that right?

ME

You represent what might have been. You started out in porn and managed to overcome it. You believe that I've already made up my mind, that I've decided to leave and nothing could convince me to reconsider. But if that was the case, then why would I be having visions of the one person who contradicts everything I've come to believe?

STAHL

You have doubts?

ME

Of course, I have doubts. I don't know if I'm making the right choice. A part of me wonders if I'd just stick it out a little longer, maybe it would all work out. If it happened that way for you, who's to say that I couldn't do it, too?

STAHL

That's a good point.

ME

But is that even what I want anymore? If I somehow managed to break through and have the writing career I always used to dream about, would it really make me happy?

STAHL

Of course, it'd make you happy. It's the American Dream. Who wouldn't want this? Who wouldn't want money and power and a creative legacy that will live on after them? What more could you ask for?

ME

I honestly don't know anymore.

STAHL

My point is, you can't give up. You can't quit. You have a responsibility to stick with it until the bitter end.

ME

And why is that?

STAHL

Don't be naive. This isn't just your life anymore. You're not the only one invested in how this turns out.

ME

I don't follow.

STAHL

You had me in the beginning. A young writer moves to Hollywood and ends up in porn. The main character isn't exactly sympathetic, but for the most part, it works. It's a classic fish-out-of-water story... but we're in the third act now, and it's starting to get depressing. We spent the entire first half watching you get beaten down. Now we want to see you win.

ME

I don't-

STAHL

No more excuses! You owe us a resolution that inspires, that gives hope. You can't let the main character walk away a loser. Where's the excitement in that?

ME

But that's not-

STAHL

Who cares if it's real? Real doesn't sell tickets. You want to end this story with a bang? *Stay* in L.A. *Don't* run away. Vanquish the forces of hypocrisy and mediocrity. Give us some reason to root for you.

ME

Well, how about if change is experienced on a smaller scale? What if, rather than conquering Hollywood, the main character just learns an important lesson about misguided ambition?

STAHL

Oh, come on, is this a goddamn after-school special? No, we need something with a little more *joie de vivre.*

ME

I'll do what I can.

Stahl grabs me by the shirt and pulls me to my feet.

STAHL

Damn right, you will. Because it's the right thing to do. The hero can't just slink out of town with his tail between his legs.

The hero always rides off into the sunset, victorious, having beaten the bad guy and gotten the girl.

ME
I'm married.

STAHL
That's the spirit.

He grips me by both shoulders and shoves me forward.

STAHL
Now, get out there. Go show those bastards what you're made of. It's time to get what you came for. Let's wrap this thing up so we can all go home.

I limp away though I'm still not sure where I'm supposed to be going and what I'm expected to do when I get there. When I look back, Stahl has vanished without a trace. I continue walking, slowly fading from view, until I am just a speck in the sand, another granule in the vast expanse of nothingness.

SLOW FADE TO BLACK

12

I was staring at the ocean. My God, I thought, what the hell is *that*? And why hadn't I noticed it before? All this time living in L.A., and not once had I seen the ocean. Not once. You'd think that such a massive body of water would have been difficult to miss.

"Keep your eyes on the road, please."

My wife sounded agitated, and she had every right to be. This detour to the beach wasn't part of the plan. I'd made a few wrong turns somewhere and taken us to the other side of the city, about as far away from the eastbound expressway as humanly possible..

"Sorry," I said, but she wasn't listening. Her face was buried in an atlas, searching for the quickest route out of town. I took one final glance towards the ocean before turning into another side street, hoping that it would eventually lead us to something resembling a major highway.

Forgive me for skipping ahead. As you might have guessed, I managed to make it home from the porn set though I can't tell you how. When the drugs finally wore off, I was somewhere just outside Malibu, walking directly through the center of rush-hour traffic. I remember being determined to finish the journey on foot. For some reason, it was extremely important. It'd been so long since I'd actually walked anywhere, I'd forgotten how liberating it could be to use your legs. If I could walk all the way home, I told myself, it would signify something. I would be purged, washed clean, a new man.

I made it as far as Santa Monica before giving up and calling for a cab.

My wife was relieved to see me, though annoyed that I hadn't gotten the check and outraged that I'd abandoned our car in Malibu. I tried to explain but the whole "drugged by a porn star" excuse sounded a little far-fetched even to me. I would have been happy just to cut our losses and find the money elsewhere but she had other ideas. In spite of all my pleading, she called Clark and arranged a visit to his office. The next day, she took a bus to the Valley and I was certain that something terrible would happen. She didn't know how these people could be. She'd say the wrong thing and they'd have her killed or worse. But in less than an hour, she returned with our car and a check that far exceeded my promised fee.

"It's over," she said. "You won't be hearing from that asshole again. I took care of *that*." She didn't offer any details and I didn't want them.

So we rented a truck, loaded it with boxes, and set off in the middle of the night. We'd originally planned to wait until morning but at the last minute, we decided to leave early. I think we both felt it would be safer this way. With each passing day, L.A. was beginning to seem more like some huge gulag. Not that we expected to find barbed-wire fences at the border but we didn't want to take any chances. It just made more sense to leave under the cover of darkness.

"Where the hell are we now?" my wife demanded.

Mistakes had been made.

"Relax, we'll get there," I said. "Besides, this is kind of nice. Think of it as a final tour of L.A. We're finally getting a chance to see all the Hollywood landmarks that we never bothered to visit while we lived here."

"I guess. It's just..." She paused, dismissed her thought with a wave.

"What?" I asked.

"It just seems like you're having second thoughts."

"About what? Leaving L.A.?"

"Well, yeah."

"Hey, this was my idea, remember?"

"Yeah, I know," she sighed. "But that doesn't mean you can't change your mind."

"Have *you* changed your mind?"

"No." She hesitated. "I mean... not really." Another pause. "It's a little late in the game for that, isn't it?"

"That's right," I said quickly, "so let's stop trying to talk ourselves out of this and find the goddamn highway."

Two hours later, we'd circled the city another dozen times and finally had to stop at a gas station to refuel the truck. My wife went inside to get coffee, and I waited in the parking lot and tried to clear my head. There was no good reason why we should still be lost. The highways were clearly marked or at least were supposed to be unless the city had conspired against us. All signs leading to the off-ramps could have been removed in a sinister plot to foil our exit. But that seemed doubtful. More than likely, this was a sabotage of our own design.

But why? What did we expect to accomplish by this pointless stalling? There was nothing left to prove here. The battle had been fought and lost. Nothing would change by driving around the city like gypsies, looking for answers that we'd never find.

I heard a muffled ringing coming from my back pocket. It sounded like my cellphone but I could have sworn that we'd canceled our service. I pulled out the phone and pounded at the keys, assuming that it was just some Pacific Bell operator calling, probably to hassle us about an unpaid bill.

When I heard the voice on the other end, my heart nearly leaped into my throat.

"Guess who?"

It was my agent.

Under different circumstances, I might have been less than delighted to hear from him. This was the man responsible for all of my recent failures. He'd promised fame and fortune, only to ignore me for months, causing a spiral of self-doubt and searing hatred for all things Hollywood. If he'd been there when I needed him, offered just a little guidance, surely it never would have come to this. I wanted to hate him and I certainly had good reason to. But I was not so jaded that I couldn't appreciate the cosmic significance in his timing.

I mean, what were the odds that he'd call me now, at the precise moment that I was on my way out of town? How could he have known? I'd never told him, never once indicated that I had any intention of leaving L.A. And what was he even doing up at such an ungodly hour? The sun had only begun to rise and most of his colleagues were only just getting out of bed for their morning lattes. It was as if he understood that time was running out. If he waited until normal business hours, it would be too late. I'd be gone, or at least out of cellphone range.

This was no coincidence. Oh no. This was nothing short of divine intervention. A higher power was at work here. I was being given a second chance. Fate had intervened in my most desperate hour. When all hoped seemed lost, I had been sent a clear signal from the universe that it had not yet given up on me.

"Listen, buddy," he said, his voice full of bubbly enthusiasm. "I'm sorry I took so long to get back to you. We've been a little crazy here."

"No problem," I said. "Don't worry about it."

"We haven't forgotten about you though. You're still our top priority."

The vision of Stahl had told me this would happen. Maybe not in so many words but he'd alluded to it. And here I thought he was just filling my head with false hope. He may have been a figment of my drug-addled imagination but he'd known that I had unfinished business. Somehow he'd known all along and I suppose, in a way, I knew it too. Why else would I have gone to such lengths to delay our departure? I'm been waiting for something, even if I didn't know what it was just yet. At least on some subconscious level, I'd expected this phone call.

"So let's talk about your screenplay," he said. "We're all very excited about it over here."

I always enjoyed the way he referred to himself in the plural, as if he was the team leader for some much larger operation. I liked the idea that he had hundreds of minions at his disposal who were, even as we spoke, working tirelessly on my behalf in an almost fanatical devotion to my career.

"We love it," he said. "The studios love it. Everybody loves it."

"That's great."

"Unfortunately, they passed."

"Who passed?"

"The studios. They said no. I'm sorry, buddy, I really am."

He said it so offhandedly, I wasn't sure how to react. If he'd at least tried to build up to the news, maybe given me some buffer against what was coming, I might have been better prepared. But he'd opted for the drive-by shooting approach, catching me completely by surprise.

"D-did they say why?" I asked, all but stuttering the words.

"Don't take this the wrong way. They're crazy about you. They think your writing's great, they think you're great, and they totally flipped for your script."

"So what's the problem?"

"They don't like the script. It's not edgy enough. I tried to talk some sense into them but they wouldn't budge. It just doesn't have that certain something they're looking for."

"Well, do they want me to rewrite it?"

"No, don't bother. It's been a weird year at the box office. *Titan A.E.* flopped and everybody is running scared. They're just not ready to take any chances right now."

There were so many things wrong with his logic, I didn't know where to begin arguing. "They're not buying my script because of *Titan A.E.*?"

"Exactly."

"An animated film about spaceships, despite the fact that my script contains neither animation nor spaceships."

"You're missing the point. Nobody's accusing you of jumping on the sci-fi bandwagon."

"I hope not. It wouldn't be true."

"But your premise does have some rather glaring similarities.

You mentioned that you were thinking about Matt Damon for the lead."

"Yeah."

"Who just so happens to be in *Titan A.E.*"

"That doesn't make any sense."

"I know, but that's the way this town thinks. It can't be helped."

"Have they even read my script?"

"Oh, please. Don't be so paranoid. I'm sure they gave it careful consideration."

A terrible thought occurred to me. "Have *you* read my script?" I asked.

"Of course I have," he said.

"Seriously?"

There was an uncomfortable pause on the other end. "Well, not the entire thing. But I read the coverage."

"What's it about?" I snarled.

"What's what about?"

"The plot. Can you summarize the plot?"

"I don't know what you're—"

"Just tell me what happens in the first scene. Or name one of the principal characters. Anything."

More silence. "Listen, I don't have time for this," he said, obviously flustered. "What's done is done. Let's move on. You need to learn how to think more pro-actively. Stop worrying about who read what and start focusing on what's important. This is about making a deal, signing your name on the dotted line, not literature appreciation."

It was as if a veil had been lifted and the great Oz exposed. I could almost hear Ray's voice reverberating through my head, like a mocking echo. "What does the fucking story have to do with anything?"

It's funny how your entire perspective can change in an instant. During my entire tenure in L.A., I never once considered myself a real Hollywood screenwriter. I just naturally assumed that I had miles to go before I could count myself among their ranks. Imagine my surprise at discovering that I hadn't been so far off after all. So I never had the money or the fame, the essence of the experience had been the same. I'd crossed the finish line long ago, I'd just never noticed until now.

"So what else have you got for me?" my agent asked.

"Excuse me?"

"Your next project. Let's set up a breakfast meeting. I have a few ideas that I'd like to run past you."

"They wouldn't happen to have anything to do with Kurosawa, would they?"

"Kurosawa? No, why would you think that? Hello? Eric? Are you still there?"

I was laughing so hard that I'd dropped the phone. I don't know what came over me. I was like some giggling Buddha who'd only just discovered that none of it mattered.

My wife returned with the coffee in time to catch me throwing our cellphone into a nearby dumpster. "What are you doing?" she asked.

"Nothing," I said. "Damn thing's broken."

"But I-"

"Let's go."

I let her drive, and we found the highway within minutes. I wanted to tell her everything but I didn't even know where to begin. How could I possibly explain? How could I find the words to make her understand?

Somewhere outside the city, I fell into a deep sleep. It was the best sleep I had all year. And this time, my dreams were pleasant, almost peaceful. I dreamt of a place far away from California. It may have been Chicago but I suppose it could have been anywhere. Hundreds of people, of every age and sex, were standing together in a single line. They were holding hands and I may be wrong but I'm pretty sure they were singing. I was struck by how ordinary they were. There was nothing particularly special about any of them. They had no apparent reason to be celebrating. but there they were, singing away, perfectly happy with their lives.

I'm not sure why I noticed this but the women in my dream were all wearing turtleneck sweaters. It may not seem like much but, to me, it was paradise.

BUTT CRAZY!

by

Eric Spitznagel

Cast List

Stacey Bright, a contestant (3 sex scenes)
Nikki Klett, a contestant (2 sex scenes)
Martha Klett, Nikki's mother (2 sex scenes)
Lloyd Burke, the pageant's founder (1 sex scene)
Francis DuBois, the choreographer (1 sex scene)
Brad, Stacey's boyfriend (1 sex scene)
Barry, a pageant judge (1 sex scene)
Raoul, a pageant judge (1 sex scene)

NON-SEXUAL ROLES

Cameraman
Dr. Marvin Leonard, cosmetic surgeon
Nurses
Boom Operator
Singer
Party Guests

SS#1: boy/girl
SS#2: boy/girl/girl
SS#3: boy/boy/girl
SS#4: girl/girl
SS#5: boy/girl

BLACK SCREEN

A title card reads:

"Last summer, (INSERT NAME OF PRODUCTION COMPANY) announced plans for the 10th annual Miss Butt USA pageant, the oldest ass beauty contest in the world. A documentary crew was hired to commemorate this historic occasion."

FADE OUT:

FADE IN:

INT. OFFICE - DAY

CLOSE on a brightly-colored publicity poster for the "MISS BUTT USA PAGEANT." The central image is a naked blonde woman, wearing a crown and pointing at her ass.

LLOYD BURKE (O.S.)
I've been with this pageant since the beginning. And you know what? There's a very good reason why we've lasted so long.

PULLING BACK, we see that this poster is hanging on the wall of an office. LLOYD BURKE sits behind his desk, speaking directly to the camera. He's an older man with gray temples and a disingenuous smile. His enthusiasm is overwhelming but infectious. His CQ reads: "Lloyd Burke, founder and president of Miss Butt USA."

LLOYD BURKE

The beauty pageant industry is an oversaturated market. You've got Miss America, Miss Universe, Miss Teen, the list goes on and on. It's hard to tell them apart anymore. That's because they're all pretty much carbon copies of each other. I mean, how many times can you watch a girl prance across a stage in an evening gown? But we stand apart because we offer something different. Your typical viewer doesn't care what a girl looks like in a sequin dress, or whether she has an opinion about apartheid. All he's interested in is her ripe, firm ass. So we've made that our specialty. We're the only beauty contest in the world that judges women solely by their butts.

INT. BEDROOM - DAY

We're in the bedroom of STACEY BRIGHT, an ambitious young girl in her early twenties. For some reason, her walls are plastered with photos of Jennifer Lopez. As we join the scene, Stacey is on her bed, lying on her stomach. She's naked from the waist down, and BRAD, her boyfriend, is rubbing an oily lotion on her butt. Her CQ reads: "Stacey Bright, contestant."

STACEY

This pageant could be a really big deal for me, y'know? If a woman has a great butt, there's no limit to what she can achieve. I mean, look at Jennifer Lopez. She makes movies and music and can date any actor she wants. She's reached the pinnacle of success. Would she have gotten all that without her fantastic ass? I don't know, but it makes you think.

CAMERAMAN (O.S.)
What is your boyfriend doing, exactly?

STACEY
Don't mind him, he's just applying my ass renewal cream. It's a moisturizing lotion that revitalizes my butt's natural sheen. This is only part of my daily ass beauty regime. Later I'll be applying a cucumber mask, a foaming cleanser, mineral powders, and vitamin C extracts.

CAMERAMAN (O.S.)
(to Brad)
Do you think Stacey has a good chance of winning the pageant this year?

BRAD
Oh fuck yeah, man. Look at her ass. It's fucking unbelievable.

STACEY
He always tells me that. He's such a sweetie.

As Brad continues to knead the lotion into Stacey's asscheeks, his face becomes flushed with excitement. He can no longer control himself, and pushes a finger into her butthole. Stacey gives him a disapproving look.

STACEY
Brad, not now. I'm being interviewed.

Brad continues to finger-fuck her, and soon she begins to enjoy it, encouraging him with slow, steady thrusts of her ass.

CAMERAMAN (O.S.)
Do you want us to leave?

Stacey says nothing, so the camera-crew stays and enjoys the show.

SEX SEQUENCE, ACTOR & ACTRESS, SS#1, B/G

INT. LIVING ROOM - DAY

We're in the living room of a typical suburban home. MARTHA and NIKKI KLETT are sitting on a couch, facing the camera. Although both women appear to be the same age, Martha is dressed like a stereotypical mother. Nikki is beautiful, in a small town America sort of way. Their CQ reads: "Nikki Klett, contestant, and mother Martha."

MARTHA
If you ask me, that Stacey Bright is a whore. Not like my Nikki. She's a good girl. And her ass is one hundred percent natural. All she has is the butt God gave her.

CAMERAMAN (O.S.)
Did you encourage your daughter to be in this pageant?

MARTHA
Well of course. This is a huge opportunity for her. Being crowned Miss Butt USA is a lot more than a fleeting moment in the spotlight. The winner also gets a scholarship, and travels around the country for public appearances. Stacey's a bright girl, but brains can only get you so far. Being an ass queen can open a lot of doors.

NIKKI

(proudly)

Did you know that my mom was the first-ever Miss Butt USA?

MARTHA

(blushes)

It's true. The pageant turned my life around. I remember it like it was yesterday. Ten years ago, I was just an innocent young thing with big dreams and a sweet ass. When I won the crown, everything changed for me. I-

CAMERAMAN (O.S.)

Excuse me, how old are you exactly?

MARTHA

Twenty-six.

CAMERAMAN (O.S.)

And your daughter?

MARTHA

Nineteen.

A long beat. Nobody says anything. It's painfully clear that the math doesn't work. Either Martha is lying, or something is very wrong here.

INT. CAR - DAY

Lloyd is behind the wheel, talking into a cellphone. He's so angry that the veins in his neck are throbbing. His calm, confident facade is beginning to fall apart.

LLOYD BURKE

I don't give a damn, we reserved that auditorium three months ago! I paid the goddamn security deposit already! Don't fucking screw me on this!

Lloyd slams the cellphone shut and throws it into the backseat. He turns to the camera and forces a smile.

LLOYD BURKE

I'm sorry you had to hear that. Organizing a pageant of this magnitude isn't easy. There are a lot of details that need to be handled. You've got to secure the location, hire the technical crew, make sure all the lighting and sound equipment is rented. It can be a major hassle. And we still haven't decided on the theme of this year's pageant. We were toying with the idea of "Butts Through History," a celebration of the most famous rumps of the millennium. You know, Marilyn Monroe, Betty Page, Martha Washington. But it lacked that certain pizzazz we're looking for.

He stares at the road, a twinkle in his eyes.

LLOYD BURKE

This year's show needs to be something extra special. It's our tenth anniversary, after all. I want it to be a real spectacle, something huge and extravagant.

INT. STAGE - DAY

A dark stage. The first few chords of "ALSO SPRACH ZARATHUSTRA" by Richard Strauss (better known as the

"Theme From 2001:A Space Odyssey") boom over the studio's sound system. Suddenly, rays of colored lights zigzag across the stage, creating a sort of man-made aurora borealis.

A single spotlight focuses our attention towards the center of the stage, illuminating Stacey's round ass.We ZOOM IN so that her butt takes up the entire screen.A tiny spaceship enters the shot, hovering over the moon-ass. It's just a plastic toy, and we can clearly see the wires used to levitate it.The spaceship lands on her butt as the music gets louder, the drums pounding violently.

FRANCIS DUBOIS (O.S.)
Cut! Cut!!

The music abruptly stops and the house lights are brought up. We PULL BACK to reveal that a TECHNICIAN is standing next to Stacey, holding a wire attached to the toy spaceship.

FRANCIS DUBOIS storms towards the stage. He's a lanky man, dressed entirely in black, with a smug, superior expression. Lloyd wanders over and stands next to the stage.

LLOYD BURKE
What's the problem, Francis?

Francis yanks the toy away from the technician, shaking it accusingly at Lloyd.

FRANCIS DUBOIS
This spaceship is only six inches long! Nobody in the audience will be able to see it!

LLOYD BURKE
It's the best we could do.

Francis massages his temples, barely able to conceal his growing fury.

FRANCIS DUBOIS
The opening number has to set the mood for the entire evening. The awe-inspiring magnificence of Man's first landing on the moon cannot be duplicated with... with... pathetic plastic toys.

LLOYD BURKE
What do you suggest?

FRANCIS DUBOIS
We need to build a moon-ass that covers the entire stage! And the spaceship must be huge, belching hot flames as it makes its glorious descent onto the lunar buttcheeks.

LLOYD BURKE
Do you have any idea what that'll cost?

Francis throws the spaceship to the ground, on the verge of a hissy fit.

FRANCIS DUBOIS
Damn the cost!

INT. BACKSTAGE - DAY

Francis is standing next to a bare wall, speaking directly to the camera. His CQ reads: "Francis DuBois, director and choreographer."

FRANCIS DUBOIS
When Lloyd first approached me about directing this year's pageant, I told him I would do it under one condition: That this would not just be another beauty contest, but a true theatrical experience. You see, I want to use this event to convey something profound and meaningful. I want to create art. I want to tell a story. And I want to do it entirely with butts.

INT. REHEARSAL SPACE - DAY

Stacey and Nikki, both naked, are lying on the cold floor, their butts faced forward. They're flexing their ass muscles, opening and closing their cheeks in regular intervals. Francis is pacing behind them, watching them closely and clicking his tongue. It's obvious that the girls are extremely intimidated by him.

FRANCIS DUBOIS
In and out. In and out. Come on, ladies! I want to see those sphincters breathing the fire of life!

FRANCIS DUBOIS (V.O.)
I've been working with the contestants for weeks, helping them choreograph their routines. But more importantly, I've tried to teach them how to use their butts as an instrument for personal expression.

Francis kneels next to Stacey and grabs her ass. He roughly massages it, staring at her butt as if hypnotized.

FRANCIS DUBOIS
Your butt is the window to your soul. Let it speak for you.

Francis has become visibly aroused by Stacey's ass. He tilts his head, as if he just heard her butt say something.

FRANCIS DUBOIS
What's that?

He leans closer and puts his ear to her butt. A beat. He listens for a moment, nodding.

FRANCIS DUBOIS
You want me to kiss you?

He turns and faces the ass, leering at it with apparent lust.

FRANCIS DUBOIS
But of course.

He kisses her butt lightly, then more forcefully. He moves down her cheeks and into her butthole. As he licks Stacey's pussy, her soft moans tells him that she's enjoying the attention.

Lloyd grabs Nikki by her ass and pulls her close. He alternates between the two girls, covering both snatches with a healthy layer of spit. They return the favor, and soon the horny threesome are having dirty sex on the floor.

SEX SEQUENCE, ACTOR & TWO ACTRESSES, SS#2, B/G/G

EXT. SIDEWALK - DAY

BARRY and RAOUL, two regular joes, are standing on a city sidewalk, facing the camera. Their CQ reads: "Barry and Raoul, pageant judges."

BARRY
Oh sure, yeah, I'm very excited about being a judge for Miss Butt USA. Weird thing is, I've had a lot of practice at this already. I've been staring at women's asses for most of my life. But most times, it ends up with me getting slapped in the face. This is the first chance I've had to get paid for doing what comes natural.

CAMERAMAN (O.S.)
How would you define the perfect ass?

RAOUL
Well, obviously, it should be plump and supple. When you slap it, it should jiggle a little. I think a good ass has its own personality. It's like, when you're looking at it, the buttcrack almost seems to be smiling at you.

BARRY
I believe rapper Sir Mix-A-Lot said it best: "I like 'em big, round and juicy."

Raoul nods thoughtfully.

The camera stays on them for just a beat too long.

EXT. BACKYARD OF STACEY BRIGHT'S HOUSE - DAY

We're watching a patio door, waiting for Stacey to join us out in the back yard.

STACEY (O.S.)
Are you ready? Here I come.

Stacey opens the door dramatically and bursts into the back yard. She struts around the lawn like she's walking down a runway, pivoting to show us every inch of her new outfit. It's a sequin dress with the ass-cheeks fully exposed.

STACEY
What do you think?

CAMERAMAN (O.S.)
Wow, that's...

STACEY
I had it made special by a top designer. It cost me a fortune but it was totally worth it. This is my outfit for the talent competition.

CAMERAMAN (O.S.)
Have you decided on a talent yet?

STACEY
(sarcastically)
Duh. I've only been working on it for a year.

CAMERAMAN (O.S.)
What is it?

STACEY

It's a magic act. I'm going to make over one hundred household objects disappear using only my butt. If you want, you can stick around and watch me practice.

She walks over to a picnic table and picks up a basket. It's filled with various items like alarm clocks, plungers, egg-beaters and candles. The cameraman's hand comes into view and picks up a stapler. He examines it with the camera lens.

CAMERAMAN (O.S.)

Are you sure this is a good idea?

STACEY

Of course it is. You can't win the Miss Butt USA pageant with some lame tap-dancing routine. You've got to give them something they'll remember. You want to help? I could use an assistant.

CAMERAMAN (O.S.)

I, uh... Where's your boyfriend?

STACEY

You mean Brad? I dumped him. I mean, he's a great guy and all. But I'm going to be a major star, and he's just holding me back. Even Jennifer Lopez dumped Ben Affleck, didn't she? And Brad is no Ben Affleck.

Stacey leans against the picnic table and lifts her butt into the air, pulling her cheeks apart with each hand. She looks back at the cameraman.

STACEY
Come on, what are you waiting for?

We TILT down to look at the stapler in our hands, then back up at Stacey's ass, then down again at the stapler. The cameraman is a little uncertain whether he wants to be a part of this.

EXT. NIKKI KLETT'S HOUSE - DAY

We're walking up the front steps to Nikki Klett's house. The cameraman's hand comes into view, and we watch him knock on the front door.

The door opens a crack and Martha Klett peers out, showing us only her face.

CAMERAMAN (O.S.)
Mrs. Klett, I was wondering if–?

MARTHA
(in a hurry)
This isn't the best time. Could you come back later?

The door slams in our face.

A beat. We wait for a moment, wondering what to do. Then we run around the side of the house, looking into various windows. Most of the rooms seem to be empty, but then we come to the kitchen. We can see Martha standing next to two men. All three of them are naked. We duck, certain that we've been spotted. But when we hear nothing, we slowly stand up and look into the window again.

We move closer, trying to get a better look. The two men with Martha are Raoul and Barry, the pageant judges we met earlier. The window is slightly ajar, so we push it open with the camera lens, moving closer to the action.

Martha is stroking the cocks of both men.

MARTHA
So I have your guarantee? You're going to vote for Nikki, right?

BARRY
Sure thing.

She falls to her knees and takes them into her mouth.

SEX SEQUENCE, TWO ACTORS & ACTRESS, SS#3, B/B/G

EXT. PARKING LOT - DAY

In the distance, we can see Lloyd walking towards his car. He looks more frazzled than usual. His hair is wild and tangled, and his suit is badly rumpled. We run towards him.

CAMERAMAN (O.S.)
Mr. Burke! Mr. Burke!

Lloyd keeps moving, speeding up to get into his car. We reach him before he manages to escape, and he shoves an open hand towards the camera lens.

LLOYD BURKE
I have no comment!

CAMERAMAN (O.S.)
Wait, Mr. Burke. It's just us.

Lloyd pulls his hand away. He straightens his tie and tries to smile for the camera. But he doesn't have the strength to pretend that everything is fine.

LLOYD BURKE
Oh, hello. Sorry about that. I've been hounded by reporters all day. This is the biggest scandal in the history of Miss Butt USA.

CAMERAMAN (O.S.)
Has Nikki been disqualified?

LLOYD BURKE
Well of course. We can't allow this sort of blatant cheating to go unpunished. I'm just happy you brought it to our attention when you did.

CAMERAMAN (O.S.)
So Mrs. Klett admitted that she bribed the judges?

LLOYD BURKE
What? No, this has nothing to do with that. I don't have a problem with mothers sleeping with our judges. We encourage that kind of behavior.

CAMERAMAN (O.S.)
But then what-?

LLOYD BURKE
That woman is not related to Nikki Klett in any way. She's just an actress. It was a deceitful attempt to win voter sympathy by posing as a former Miss Butt Beauty Queen. This is the sort of bad publicity that could irrevocably tarnish the good reputation of our pageant.

INT. NIKKI KLETT'S BEDROOM - DAY

Nikki is in tears. She's sitting on her bed, which is covered in crumbled tissues. Next to her is Martha, her "mother."

NIKKI
I'm just so embarrassed. I didn't know we were doing anything against the rules. I just...

Nikki bursts into tears. Martha looks at the camera with a guilty expression.

MARTHA
It's my fault. I'm the one who came up with the idea. If anybody here is to blame, it's me.

NIKKI
Don't say that. You were just trying to help.

CAMERAMAN (O.S.)
Do you feel you've been treated unfairly?

NIKKI
I do, actually. I'm not the only one in this pageant cheating.

CAMERAMAN (O.S.)
What do you mean?

NIKKI
Well, Stacey Bright has her own dirty little secret. Her butt is totally fake. She's had so much reconstructive surgery, I wouldn't be surprised if her ass was made entirely out of foam rubber.

Nikki begins to cry again.

NIKKI
I can't believe it's over. I really thought I could win this year.

MARTHA
It's okay, sweetie. We still have each other.

They kiss each other gently, first on the cheek and then moving toward their mouths. As their kissing becomes more passionate, they begin pulling at each other's clothes, exposing their ample bosoms.

BOOM OPERATOR (O.S.)
Let's go. We need to confirm this Stacey Bright story.

We turn to leave. The BOOM OPERATOR is standing next to the door, waiting for us. But then we PAN back to the two girls. They're now naked and caressing each other. We PAN back to the boom operator, who is urging us to join him.

BOOM OPERATOR
Are you coming?

We PAN back to the girls, who are fingering each other's pussies. We're going to stay and watch these girls fuck. To hell with serious reporting, this is more fun.

SEX SEQUENCE, TWO ACTRESSES, SS#4, G/G

INT. OPERATING ROOM - DAY

A surgery is in progress. DR. MARVIN LEONARD, dressed in white scrubs, is standing over his PATIENT. The patient is lying face down on an operating table, her body concealed by a white sheet with a hole cut out for the ass. NURSES stand nearby, handing the doctor various surgical instruments. His CQ reads: "Dr. Marvin Leonard, cosmetic surgeon."

DR. MARVIN LEONARD
Stacey Bright? Sure, I remember her. She was a patient of mine not too long ago. As I recall, her ass was flat as a pancake. So I gave her a complete butt lift and augmentation.

CAMERAMAN (O.S.)
What's that, exactly?

DR. MARVIN LEONARD
It's a fairly simple procedure. I'm in the middle of one right now. We use a state-of-the-art butt implant, which is inserted directly into the ass.

He holds up a "butt implant" for the camera. It seems to be nothing more than a balloon filled with water.

DR. MARVIN LEONARD
It's surprisingly lifelike. Most people can't tell the difference. As I recall, Stacey was so pleased with the results that she returned for eighteen more implants. Her butt is now almost completely man-made.

CAMERAMAN (O.S.)
Is it safe?

DR. MARVIN LEONARD
(laughs)
Of course. This is the most scientifically-advanced butt technology available. There's no chance that-

The implant in Dr. Leonard's hands bursts, and water spills out onto the patient. A beat. The doctor stares helplessly at the empty implant. Slowly, he looks back at the camera.

DR. MARVIN LEONARD
You're not going to include this part, right?

INT. LLOYD BURKE'S HOUSE/ LIVING ROOM - NIGHT

A party is in progress. GUESTS are huddled together in small groups throughout the house, drinking champagne and talking quietly. A stereo plays in the background. A huge banner hangs on the wall. It reads: "MISS BUTT USA: Better Luck Next Year!"

We wander through the party, looking for Lloyd Burke. We finally find him at the bar, pouring himself a large glass of gin (obviously not his first of the evening). His clothes are in disarray, his face unshaven, and his eyes betray a defeated spirit. He turns to us, nods, and downs his drink in one swallow.

LLOYD BURKE
As I'm sure you've heard by now, we've had to cancel the pageant.

CAMERAMAN (O.S.)
What? I don't understand.

Lloyd pours himself another glass of gin.

LLOYD BURKE
After we learned about Stacey's butt enhancements, we also discovered that almost every contestant was in some way violating the rules of Miss Butt USA. A few girls were caught using butt steroids. At least three admitted to varnishing their butts with shellac to make them extra shiny. We even found out that one of them wasn't a real woman.

He shudders, nauseated by the thought. He swallows his gin in one gulp and begins to pour another.

CAMERAMAN (O.S.)
So now what?

LLOYD BURKE
Well, since everybody has been disqualified, we can no longer hold an official ceremony. But as this is the anniversary of Miss

Butt USA, it seems a shame not to pick a new queen anyway. So we've decided to try something a little different this year.

CAMERAMAN (O.S.)
What's that?

LLOYD BURKE
The first former contestant to come to my house and have sex with me will receive the crown.

The doorbell rings. Lloyd walks over to the front door and opens it. Stacey Bright is standing there, gasping for breath and holding the door frame for support. She must have run all the way here.

Lloyd turns and addresses the guests.

LLOYD BURKE
We have a winner!

The crowd cheers.

INT. LLOYD'S BEDROOM - MINUTES LATER

We're witnessing the unofficial Miss Butt USA crowning ceremony. Stacey is kneeling on all fours on Lloyd's bed, her ass propped in the air. As Lloyd slowly approaches her with the crown, a SINGER performs the Miss Butt USA victory theme song.

SINGER

(sings)

There she is! Miss Butt USA! She's so lovely! An ass straight from heaven!

Lloyd places the crown on Stacey's ass. The crowd, which is standing nearby, applauds wildly. Stacey waves to her adoring public, her face still out of view. Lloyd quickly disrobes, and begins eating out Stacey from behind. After a heart-stopping bout of foreplay, they fuck like greased weasels.

SEX SEQUENCE, ACTOR & ACTRESS, SS#5, B/G

FADE TO BLACK

About the Author

Eric Spitznagel has been a professional writer and humorist for well over a decade. He's the author of four humor books: *Planet Baywatch: The Unofficial Guide to the New World Order* (St. Martin's), *A Guy's Guide to Dating* (Doubleday), *Cigar Asphyxianado* (Warner Books), and *The Junk Food Companion: A Celebration of Eating Badly* (Plume). Believe it or not, a few of those are still in print. He's also written for hundreds of magazines, including *Playboy, Esquire, Spy, Blender, Harper's, McSweeney's* and *Salon.com*. He's currently an editor at *The Believer* magazine.

After fleeing Los Angeles, he returned to Chicago and began teaching comedy writing for the world-famous Second City Theater. He also penned dozens of plays that were produced by people with access to storefront theaters. His personal favorites were "Romeo & Juliet Died for Our Sins" and "Nothing Cute Gets Eaten," if only because he thinks the titles were kinda clever. Since then, he and his wife have lived in Sonoma, California, the woods of northern Michigan and, most recently, Salt Lake City, Utah. No, he's not a Mormon, thanks for asking. Though he has managed to stay away from the porn business, he has agreed to co-author Ron Jeremy's autobiography, forthcoming from HarperCollins.

Acknowledgments

In no particular order, the author owes a debt of gratitude to Kelly Kreglow, Amy Güth, Litsa Dremousis, Bret Scott, Tim Bennett, Mark and Lynn Spitznagel, Ron Jeremy, Josh Behar, Bob Larkin, Stephen Randall, Dan Mandel, Kelly Schaffer, Jennifer Joseph, Kevin Sampsell, "Satchmo," and everybody at *The Believer* magazine. You know why.